Raqs to Riches

DANCE WITH PASSION, ACHIEVE SUCCESS

BY ORIANA BROOKS

ISBN: 978-0-359-90073-2

For Patty, Karissa and Liz.

Never stop asking questions.

A FOREWORD BY TAMALYN DALLAL

Oriana's new book, "Raqs to Riches: Dance with Passion, Achieve Success," at first glance seems like a comprehensive guide for students and dancers who are breaking into the performing arena. As the book progresses, I realize that there is a lot that seasoned dancers can gain from this book. It covers a lot of ground, as if she is writing everything she wished someone would have told her over the years. Now she is sharing all of this with you.

Each chapter has questions and exercises that can help one better understand their own reasons for dancing, their motives and what makes them find joy and satisfaction in the dance.

Through this book, aspiring dancers can learn how to avoid some of the pitfalls along the way.

I love how Oriana shows how to manifest, visualize and develop an alter ego, which may sound romantic, but her approaches are very practical.

Then she gives pointers on marketing, show structure, salesmenship, website design and other nitty gritty information I wish I knew when I was starting out.

"Raqs to Riches" is full of stories and anecdotes that, while entertaining, also give us good ideas. Oriana names one of the techniques for improvisation after one of her teachers, Najmah. She calls it the

"Najmah Technique." Not only do you get good advice from Oriana, but she gives credit to her teachers as well.

She discusses the difference between being an excellent teacher and an excellent performer, which may or may not go hand in hand. Yet, if one chooses to teach, chapter 5 in this book gives plenty of guidance.

This book is well thought out, from years of teaching. There is a lot of positivity and motivation, but also reality checks, so newer dancers have some idea of what to expect as they get into the world of dance, and how to deal with the moments that can be scary or disappointing. Orianas advice can help a dancer avoid being scarred by some of the negative aspects and move on to an abundance of positive and happy experiences.

INTRODUCTION FROM THE AUTHOR

When I was a little girl, I used to get so excited when my parents would get ready to go out and play music. I would pretend to be asleep in the late hours of the night while my dad put on his fancy clothes and my mom curled her hair. She used to wear a perfume that she whould only wear when she would go out to perform. It was called Xia Xiang. I didn't know at the time that it was a fairly inexpensive perfume and I still don't care if it was. It was heavy and musky and my little kid mind thought it was a magic potion that gave my mom the power to get up on stage and sing at her piano.

Playing music was also the only time my mom wore lipstick and a black velvet jacket, and my dad wore a hat. Any other time of the week we were eating dollar store macaroni and cheese and my father took his heart meds.

Performing is a magical thing. It's crazy, slightly insane and a whole lot of fun if you play your cards right. I never in a million years thought I would grow up to be a professional Bellydancer but the love of the stage is engrained in me. However, it's not for sissies. When I first started my mom asked if I needed an agent. I laughed a little and said, "Mom, there's Facebook now!" Her face went blank. "So, you're doing your own booking??"

The entertainment industry is a fast paced swirl where it's easy to get lost in the moment and forget what it was you wanted to do anyway. It takes a lot of work to get noticed, get ahead and get paid.

This book is the culminative product of my inquisitive students, the perfromers I have mentored and my studies as a Confidence Coach. It is a healthy dose of reality, the Law of Attraction and my own personal flavor of snarky humor.

My hope is that it will be a handy and easy to use guide throughout your career.

May the wings of your eyeliner be always even. May your coffee be strong and your love of this ancient artform be even stronger. Inch'allah.

Table of Contents

CHAPTER ONE

Why Do We Dance?

It's a legitimate question. Of all of the things that we can and cannot supposedly do, why do we choose to spend our time and energy in a practice that is steeped in stigma, mystery and ever-evolving technique. Truly, Bellydance in America attracts a particular kind of person. Sorjourners of sensual truth and students searching for belonging among others like themselves. Does our desire for dance and drums stem from an ancient tribal need for communal experience or does it go deeper?

Movement is addicting! Pulsing inside nightclubs and living in professional dance studios exists the sovereign truth: movement and music are the parents of FUN. Human emotion flows from our interactions with movement. The first dance at a wedding, high school proms, Saturday nights out with friends, the living human mass of waving arms at a rock concert and even those silly line dances that no one seems to like but everyone knows anyway.

There is no denying the power of a thumping drum beat and our brains being bathed in a euphoric chemical cocktail. There are levels to everything however, and much like the seasons some of us bloom past spring and go into summer to become professional dancers.

Blossoming on a tree made of discipline and sweat after spending years (and hundreds of dollars) on classes, workshops, costumes and travel- Bellydancers are a rather impassioned bunch. Each one of us is slightly different and unique and perhaps that is the biggest reason we are attracted to such a complex artform. We value uniqueness. We reason that are the free spirits and the gypsy souls that turn against the tide of mediocrity to defiantly roll our hips in joyous rebellion as we share our space with a sisterhood of swiling skirts and the endless tinkling of zills and glittering hip scarves.

Right?

I am reminded of my personal high school experience. My freshman class began with a little over 900 students. That's a lot! However, by the time we all got to graduation there were only 323 of us left standing to switch our tassels to the other side. Yes, two-thirds of my original class had switched schools, moved, or simply dropped out. Each year experienced a whittling down of population until at last by the fourth year we all finally knew each other well enough to feel a sense of community.

So too it is with any practice. Some students will take the exits off the Bellydance highway to hobby-ville or fitness city, some drive a little further and get off at Semi Pro-land and so on. Some of us push and push and push until we run out of highway to drive on and have to begin off-roading in the woods. Middle Eastern Dance is not your average highway either; there are way more exits than destinations and far more academic off-shoots than most people care to explore in their lifetimes. I've had far more students coming to class to keep fit and have fun than to train to become elite competitive dancers. However, I've had a significant enough amount of dance students suddenly realize that somehow they had veered far off the course of their heart's desire and wound up bored; paying for classes they didn't enjoy and rehearsing for shows they didn't want to be in.

Where is your Bellydance highway taking you to? This is normally when most people insert a very motivational quote regarding each person having their own journey and their own path down their own widning road with their own unique vision about their own life.

I'm not one to say any part of that statement is wrong per se.... but I am going to say that both the hobbyist and the serious student should put more thought into what they would like their Bellydance journey to morph into. Instead of throwing our hip belts to the wind and writing off every performance, song choice and decision as a mere pebble on our little wooded personal paths; consider investing the time into planning your dance life like you would do your normal life. Setting goals, timelines, deadlines and even vision boards can be extermely powerful tools for getting the most out of your time in class. A little piognacy can be extremely prudent when it comes to choosing teachers, which fields of study you may further yourself in and what type of performances you do. Remember the old adage, "An ounce of prevention is worth a pound of cure?" Drawing up some ideas now can prevent buyer's remorse later!

Let's begin. You'll want to keep some spare paper and pen handy. I recommend writing these answers in whatever journal or notebook you keep your other dance notes in.

You will probably think I am the lamest teacher ever but I will admit to you I've taken a lot of my personal business training and counseling techniques as inspiration to form the following questions. I can tell you from personal experience the largest turning points in my dance career came from using business and marketing techniques to orient myself towards my highest potential. I know, I know. It's not covered in glitter and coins. I know, I know. That's the BORING world. Humor me and you'll see the method in the madness. These questions are designed to establish your home base of where you see yourself now, and where you might see yourself going in the future as a dancer. Answer honestly, vivdly and impulsively (no one needs to see this but you). Going with your gut reponse is one of the best favors you can do for yourself and you might just be surprised with what you come up with!

Think about the last time you performed a bellydance number. Close your eyes and begin to recall the feelings, sensations, scents and who you talked to. How did you feel before, during and after?

1.   The last time I performed was _____ for _____. Afterwards, I felt_____ because _____.

Three things I felt I did well were:

Three things I believe could use improving are:

2. If I had an unlimited source of money, with unlimited free time, the ability to travel anywhere including back in time I would choose to study with these teachers:

3. My dream costume is _____ with _____ and _____ and made by _____.

4. I feel like I need more help with _____.

5. My favorite prop is_____ but I'd also like to try _____ some day.

6. The last time I felt really excited about dance was when_____.

7. The last time I watched another dancer and couldn't keep my eyes off of them was_____.   What struck me about their performance was_____.

8. The last time I watched another dancer and didn't like the performance was_____ because _____.

9. I've always been curious about _____ style, because _____.

10. If dance were the only thing I had to do for the rest of my life, I believe my ultimate goal would be to _____.

That wasn't so bad now, was it? In fact, I wager that your brain is probably jumping up and down with curiosity and wonder. Or, maybe it's even a little nostalgic. Did you have a few answers surprise you? Were some of the questions harder than others?

These questions should have given you a pretty good idea of where your inner dancer is pulling you to go, and also what you may like to avoid. If you've begun to feel a little down on yourself with regret for not accomplishing some of these ideas earlier on: hold your horses. Resist the terriffic urge to slap yourself on the wrist for not buying that costume, not going to that class, doing that show you didn't want to do or forgetting about that veil in the closet. You are human. You are here, now, redirecting the course of your intention towards what will make your heart sing. And that's something to feel good about. There is no time limit on the journey to joy.

Another neat side effect of this exercise is that once you have declared in your mind what you want to start doing, seeing and experiencing; you will actually begin to mysteriously start seeing, doing and experiencing those things! The Law of Attraction has made this seemingly magic premise into popular thought but it is also still refrerred to by it's older name coined by Dr. Carl Jung- "Synchronicity." (insert quote and reference here)

Synchronicity is not a magician's hat, however. You don't simply think of new zills and suddenly they appear on your doorstep like the tooth fairy came by. Rather it's better to think of these questions as grooming your brain to begin to really clearly recognize what you are looking for amidst the noise of everyday life. Let's say, for example, you wrote down that you really do need a new pair of zills. What kind of zills? Well, the kind you saw that one lady use at that one show that one time, duh. They were smaller and kind of silver looking, but they sounded like little bells and were quite pleasant.

So now you have an abstract idea of what you're looking for. Your next steps could be to ask your teacher what kind of zills those could be, or perhaps to start looking up zills online and see if any match the description of what you remember (the really good company websites also provide sound clips of the zills they sell). Now we're off to the races. Having acquired more information on the zills you were thinking of you can now choose your own adventure. Find and buy the ones your remember OR end up finding even better ones OR (the most miraculousof all) a pair of zills will seemingly materialize into your life. This actually happened to me on one occasion. When I was still a green dancer I realized I should get a pair of zills because I was looking into dancing at resturants. Within one week I had been gifted THREE pairs of zills from random coworkers and friends. The craziest part was that I hadn't even told them I was thinking about! Can you imagine if I had?

Here's another great example; the thought- "I really need harder classes, I like my teacher but I'm bored." Writing prompt answer- "If I had my choice to study with anyone I would definately pick Mary Sue Dancer. I saw a video of her once and I was stunned. But, she lives in Canada." Next thought- "I'll look at her website, maybe she'll tour near me some day. Oh look! She does online live classes! I CAN study with her!" Again, this actually happened to me. That is synchronicity in motion. When you go for what you really feel good about, it's like the Universe joins in and hands you a voucher. Thoughts lead to actions and actions lead to results. The Dance Universe is just waiting for you to take the first step.

Further Thoughts:

Can you think of times in your dance career that it seemed like fate, kismet, or just a little more than coincedence? What part did you play in helping that happen? Remembering times when our actions lead to good things helps us remember we still hold the Captain's Wheel to our own ships when we feel a little lost at sea.

CHAPTER TWO

Get A Plan, Stan.

———————◦———————

A major mistake I see most advancing dance students make, aside from not having a plan at all, is thinking that they must stick to a specific plan no matter what. They mentally sign an irrevocable contract with themselves gauranteeing that they will either be a non-famous complete beginner their entire lives or they must push themselves to the brink of complete exhaustion believing they must follow the same path as their heroes or teachers.

Over and over again I've students across multiple genres and and levels turn down opportunities because they pigeonhole their abilities or utterly overload themselves and self-sabotage because they take on every oppotunity regardless style, financial cost and so on. Trust me when I say that both scenarios are equally as detrimental.

I like to tell my students that performing is like dating. Before you begin to date, you are most likely single and have some sort of routine in your lifestyle. You eat take-out two times a week, go to yoga on Tuesdays and have your usual running paths determined. You decide one day after a 7 hour Netflix marathon that you would like to meet someone. Before you begin dating, you've most likely fantasized about what kind of relationship you'd like; their personality, hobbies, appearance and sun sign. Then as you start dating you begin to filter out who meets most of those traits and who isn't a good fit for you. Sometimes this is tumultuous but you get the idea. The goal is to meet someone who meets most of your requirements while having traits that are tolerable even if they aren't on your list. Your partner should enhance your life, not make it harder.

Bellydance should be the same way! Your performances, teachers, costumes and social circle should enhance your life and career. If you are closed off to opportunity you deny the ability to enhance your life with newness and wonder. If your career is too chaotic and you never focus on any direction whatsoever enhancement will never come because there will be no advancement. Closed doors mean no journey: the hermit or princess locked in the tower. Forcing or keeping too many open doors means a maze of unfinished projects and underdeveloped ideas. Jack of many trades, master of none as the saying goes.

The questions in Chapter One touched on some of these thoughts but now let's dig deeper. Let's be honest, there is a time in every student's experience when they realize their "style" is solely because of the influence of their most prominent teacher. Like a child developing a sense of the world for the first time, a dancer can start to look elsewhere and it sometimes feels overwhelming at first. There are so many styles and so much information to filter as well as questionable resources prolifically arguing on social media.

Know that you won't have the answers all at once. If your destiny is to advance very far into Middle Eastern Dance then your career will be a rather scholarly pursuit rife with just as much history and anthropology training as much as actual dance training. If your destiny is to be an organizer of events, your career will branch off into marketing, finances and communications.

This chapter is more of a personality test than anything. I believe every advancing Bellydancer falls into at least one of these archetypal positions: The Life Long Learner, The Traveler, The Professor, The Organizer, the Assistant and the Showgirl.

You may be looking over that list and already thinking you fit into at least one or more. That's a good sign and very normal! Having a intuitive sense of self points towards your capabilities and desires. The following is a fun personality test of hypthetical situations that will help you determine what you most likely fit into. Remember, your values and reponses may change over time. Feel free to come to this again and again as needed.

Circle the letter of the response that most closely fits you. Yes, you can only pick one. Try to think of real life scenarios that you experienced and choose the answer that is closest to what you actually did.

1. You realize that you have extra vacation days at work and decide that you want to spend them on something dance related. You begin:
    a. to look for conventions and workshops and schedule your time off based on them.
    b. to consider what city or country you'd like to visit and coordinate which dancers or studios you'll meet up with while you're there.

    c.   to plan to set aside time during your vacation to finally finish a choreography you've been working on and bring books and music to enjoy no matter where you go.

    d.   to plan an informal hafla with your best dance gal pals to catch up and dance at the same time!

    e.   to email your teacher and ask if you can help out or can arrange for work study at a show for you.

    f.   to fervently look for bookings or shows to drop into while you're off work.

2.   Lucky day! You find $20 in an old jacket pocket. What do you spend it on?

    A.   Music, yoga pants or hip scarves.

    B.   cell phone chargers, new headphones or a new gig bag.

    C.   Journals, Camera stand, or online lectures/lessons.

    D.   New business cards/ advertising material, decor, or FB ads.

    E.   Planner, dress clothes, or office supplies.

    F.   Makeup, manicure or cute cell phone case.

3.   Your old cell phone has finally bitten the dust. What's the most important function you are looking for as you shop for a new one?

    A.   plenty of storage space for music and video files and good sound qaulity

    B.   Plenty of space for pictures, access to cloud storage and has excellent coverage

    C.   supports all of your organizational apps and has a built in voice activated assistant

D. supports every social media app known to man for advertising your shows

E. nice large screen for video messaging and filming

F. can hold all of your photo editing apps, photos and music

4. You're catching up with your best dance friend. What are you most likely to talk about?

A. This awesome workshop you took last weekend.

B. How much you're loving the new rideshare programs

C. A new project you're working on or the most interesting podcast you heard the other day about obscure arabic rhythms

D. A new charity event you're thinking of hosting

E. The mishaps at the last show you helped with

F. The funny things that happened at the last show you performed in

5. From these options, what type of car would you choose and why?

A. A sensible fuel efficient hatchback because I drive all over the place for lessons and haflas

B. Something I could spend the night in ideally, like a tour bus or a camper.

C. An easy going sedan with low payments and bluetooth is mandatory for messages and students calling

D. A crossover vehicle that has plenty of room for merchandise, props and music equipment

E. A comfortable car that everyone can fit in, with room for decorations!

F.   An economic car that is still easy on the eyes and has plenty of room for gear. I use Uber for everything else.

6.   What does your bellydance music library look like?

A.   A little bit of everything, some classic, some fusion, dubstep, top 40 and a lot of songs I shazam'd in class!

B.   multiple playlists of sets, oragnized by country and some meditations for long rides

C.   Class playlists, rhythm samples, music from nearly every era and some fusion just for good measure

D.   lots of intrumentals for background music, as well as backups for everyone's songs that they submitted!

E.   A hodge podge of different songs I've heard at shows and in classes over the years. I don't perform much, so it's whatever I like at the time.

F.   All of the classics. Drum solos and pre made set lists so I'm ready to go!

Now let's look at your answers!

If you answered:

Mostly A's- you are The Life Long Learner

You have the most fun in the classroom! You are constantly looking for, and attending, classes of all types. Being active in workshops is your idea of being involved and you may not necessarily feel that professional performing is right for you. Your joy stems from knowledge gained and being able to experience new styles with others. You are most likely the type of person to take lessons in a little bit of everything and all of your friends are at the studio for the ultimate girl's night every time you go!

Mostly B's- The Traveler

You are most likely the dancer that loops conventions, performances and workshops in conjunction to your vacations. To you, half the fun of dance is being able to travel and explore! Meet new people, see the sights, road trips and baggage claims. Bellydance is your way to "get away from it all." You might even dream of touring one day or have a bucket list of festivals you'd like to attend. You are most likely the dancer that enjoys the total separation of dance from your everyday life.

Mostly C's- The Professor

You may already be a teacher/studio owner or might be thinking of becoming one. The Professor takes Bellydance to a more academic route, and your dance practice will most likely include more culture and history studies than other dancers. Unlike the Life Long Learner, you absorb this knowledge not just for fun but rather to relay to others later. You are most likely the type of dancer to drawn towards mentorship, coaching and giving advice to others.

Mostly D's- The Organizer

Life is a party that you are hosting! Your contribution to the dance community is organizing and holding different shows, haflas or charity events. You are drawn to either bringing people together or the actual organizing process, or both! You may even be drawn to social action or benefits that bring the dance community to larger current events. You believe things are always better, more fun and way more beneficial with everyone on board!

Mostly E's- The Assistant

You're a backstage kind of person, someone who loves the details and hands on work of stage managing, filming, admin work, and sometimes subbing class.....without the nitty gritty of being the Organizer or full-time Professor. You love lending a hand and being involved. You are the support team and feel satisfaction at your contribution to the overall process. You don't mind getting your hands dirty and want to see a job done right. You are most likely the dancer that is pinning someone's costume in the dressing room or answering phone calls at the desk before class.

Mostly F's- the Showgirl

This is the category that most dancers believe they will fall into, but surprise! Not everyone is, or has to be, a dedicated 100% 24/7 showgirl. This type of dancer lives and breathes the show life. If it doesn't get them on stage, they question if it is worth the trouble. Or, the majority of their intentions are aligned towards use in performing. The ultimate goal may not be fame (although that is likely a side goal) but instead financial compensation or being able to perform in different shows. The difference between the Life Long Learner and the Organizer from the Showgirl is that the Showgirl's purpose and intention are geared towards professional recognition and achievement.

As of ____(date)____ I believe myself to be _____(type of dancer)_____.

Take a moment and consider what your result was. If you feel at ease or even happy with your result, you are on the right track! Advanced dancers may be feeling a little confused; you might see yourself in multiple categories or have done them in the past. I personally feel this is normal. The studio owner, for example, will wear many hats ranging from teacher to hafla organizer to being her own bookkeeper. I do also believe, however, one of these archetypes will resonate the most powerfully in your heart and that is the quality to never ever lose sight of. Knowing your true passion within the larger context of the dance will guide your decisions and help you find your way back home should you meander off your path for a while.

I would be remiss if I did not mention some of the negative qualities to watch for with each of these archetypes. You might have even read over the descriptions with a chuckle, knowing full well it was a little too positive and you've encountered that type and by golly they were a real jerk to be around!

First and formost let's get one really big, unpopular, hairy fact out of the way.

Not everyone will get along.

I'll be going over how to handle some of the stickier situations in a later chapter but for now let's just establish that every one has different opinions, outlooks, world views and modes of thought. Inevitably, we all at some time will butt heads over differences of values. The Showgirl will most likely not appreciate the student hafla that the Organizer is hosting, and the Life Long Learner will not want to be pressured into being the Showgirl. This is simply (albeit in a convoluted way sometimes) due to differences of core values. We all may have the wonderful qulities listed above, but for each type of dancer, and furthermore each individual there will be core values that we simply will not budge on. Rare is the dancer that never has any conflict in their career. Especially if their career is advancing past that of a hobbyist.

Now for the aforementioned negative qualities. Or, as most teachers would prefer to call them, "Opportunities:"

The Lifelong Learner

Always the Bridesmaid and never the Bride. Pushing yourself outside of your comfort zone can do you a world of good sometimes, you know. There is a tendency for this type of dancer to have "all or nothing" thinking. The studio hafla will not turn you into a hairy beastly Diva that demands champagne in her room nor will it require you to persue stardom and go on a world tour.

Another, more common, situation I've seen come up for this type is feeling pressured to stay in a studio in which they are unhappy or bored. They have so many ties and friendships at the studio that they feel guilty for looking for lessons elsewhere. You have permission to explore what would make you truly happy.

The Traveler-

I'll be frank. The biggest issue with Travelers is that they don't always understand why everyone isn't one! This can lead to feelings of loneliness or resentment towards others. Life is one convention or festival after another for you. Remember to have a little compassion for your friends that live vicariously through your Instagram feed between 2am baby feedings and on their 30 min lunch breaks. Better yet, remember to explore your own backyard every once in a while and reconnect with the normal studio goers. It'll keep you grounded and remind you of life outside of Bellydance-Land.

The Professor-

Professors have a tendency to get overwhelmed and burnt out. We are the business entreprenuers, the researchers, the paper writers and the life coaches. (Notice how I said "we?" Guilty as charged.) Self care is essential, if somewhat hard to fit in, for these types even if they are not professional teachers as they are most likely to be the ones that everyone turns to for help. Schedule down time and find things that are not dance related to enjoy. Succesful Professors often have a small side hobby to recharge with before going back to answering student messages.

The Organizer-

The Organizer's biggest challenge is attempting the nearly impossible task of bringing together members of all the other archetypes without incident. Already usually being people pleaser's or wanting admiration from others, Organizer's first hard lesson is that is exceedingly difficult to please everyone all of the time. This can be emotionally damaging and the stress can bring out the worst in them (I say this with compassion, organizing and producing events is hard work and expensive). In some rarer cases Organizer's believe they should be socially revered because they are creating events and view other events as competition. Heed these words oh mighty event host: Not everyone will care. Not everyone will want to play the game. And there will be other events. Do events for the right reasons and hold on to that. Maintaining healthy relationships and a good support network will help deter the feeling that people are ganging up on you.

The Assistant-

Assistants tend to be quiet and have work horse ethics. They will stay until the job is done and take on more tasks if asked. So at some point, their limits will be tested by someone making too many demands of them. I suspect if you are this type you've already had some late nights at the studio where you stayed way longer than you planned much to the dismay of your family or you've already ended up bringing your "volunteering" home with you! Be insistent that you have your limits and guard them. There is a big difference between volunteering and sacrifice. You are not everyone's personal assistant and you have your own life to tend to. Even if you really enjoy helping out, remember that never saying NO can you make you one grumpy little worker bee. That's no fun at all.

The Showgirl-

Yes, Showgirls have the stigma of being the Diva, the self-righteous glamourous egotistical performer that must be center stage. But I know what it really is. It's self imposed and/or outside pressure. If you are on the verge (or in the midst of) having meltdowns over things you can't control like the venue's sound equipment or two extra pounds of water weight then ask yourself: Is this because I feel the pressure to be perfect all the time? Is this because I feel financial pressure and I'm afraid I'll lose bookings? Is this because I don't have much of a regular social life? Learn to release the often perceived and not real pressure of being flawless at all times and take care of your home life first. You cannot control how often you will be booked and the rate of interest in Bellydances ebbs like the tides. Taking time to sort out your feelings, finances and relationships now will save the rest of us from having to deal with your cranky resentful self later. (Not to mention that when you feel secure, you'll be an even better performer because your mind will be at ease.)

Let's check in.

How are you feeling right now? Are you beginning to understand that the world of the advancing dancer is more than what meets the eye? When you decide to do anything seriously and with commitment the multitude of facets in your "regular" life will be affected for better or for worse. Snags in your personal life will suddenly rear their ugly little heads and seemingly pop up at the very worst times. You may already know this from other challenges you've already experienced or even from other self-help books you've read. But trust me when I say that the absolute worst time for what seemed like a minor personal irritant or outside issue to overwhelm you is when you're about touch the stage. I actually put my phone away before a show these days. The amount of sour texts and emails I've gotten right before a performance is too embarassing to count. You don't need to know about your overdraft fees as your music starts to play.

Any performer no matter the genre will tell you that when you are about to perform time stops. For the length of your time in the spotlight there cannot be anything else. It is freeing and truly unexplainable. It's like entering another dimension- a space where time holds still and that will be immortalized in photo and video. The mind focuses to razor sharp acuity and the eyes are blinded by the giant lights hovering above you. Hours, days and sometimes weeks of preparation come down to this fleeting moment of just trying to get it as right as possible. I theorize this is why most dancers really do consider dance a sport.

It is so important, especially for budding performers, to have goals. Little goals, medium sized goals, lofty goals Incredibly seemingly impossible and itsy bitsy tiny goals. Goals with timelines, dreamy goals, goals for the next performance. You get the idea. The best thing about goals? They can CHANGE as you reach them!

At one point in my early career it was absolute goal to become a restaurant dancer. I really thought that was the pinnacle at the time. And why wouldn't I? Real costume, live music, actual pay. Not to mention the teachers I admired were all resturant dancers on the weekends. So I pursued that goal relentlessly, and finally acheived it. However as time passed it became clear through soul-searching and circumstances that I was really destined to be a teacher and fell in love with traditional Egyptian styles. Once I understood that, all of my goals since have been in line with just that. My Goals shifted to study with Egyptian teachers, goals to write choreography, goals to produce shows featuring traditional dances, so on and so on.

There is absolutely no written-in-stone requirement that you must set ONE goal on your very first try and that is all you can ever achieve. I feel that this concept is widely accepted in our regular lives but somehow becomes skewed when we become dance students. I've seen too many people burdoned with the idea, as I once was, that there is only one path to acheive greatness as a dancer.

The Key to writing goals is to make them specific and with a deadline. For Example, "I will have two new costumes that I can use on a professional stage by the end of Fall." as opposed two "I want two more costumes." Intention is a very powerful mental trigger. Once you set your goals your brain begins to process your immediate environment at all times to search for what you asked for like a bloodhound on the trail. You may wish to print this list out, create a vision board out of it or simply keep it in a place where you can see it often.

Write three goals you have for your dance within the next month:

Write three goals you have for your dance within the next three months:

Write two goals you have for your dance within the next six months:

What is your biggest goal for this year?:

Write a music goal:

Write a costume goal:

Write a choreography goal:

Who will help you with these goals?:

How will you achieve these goals?:

Why are these goals important to you?:

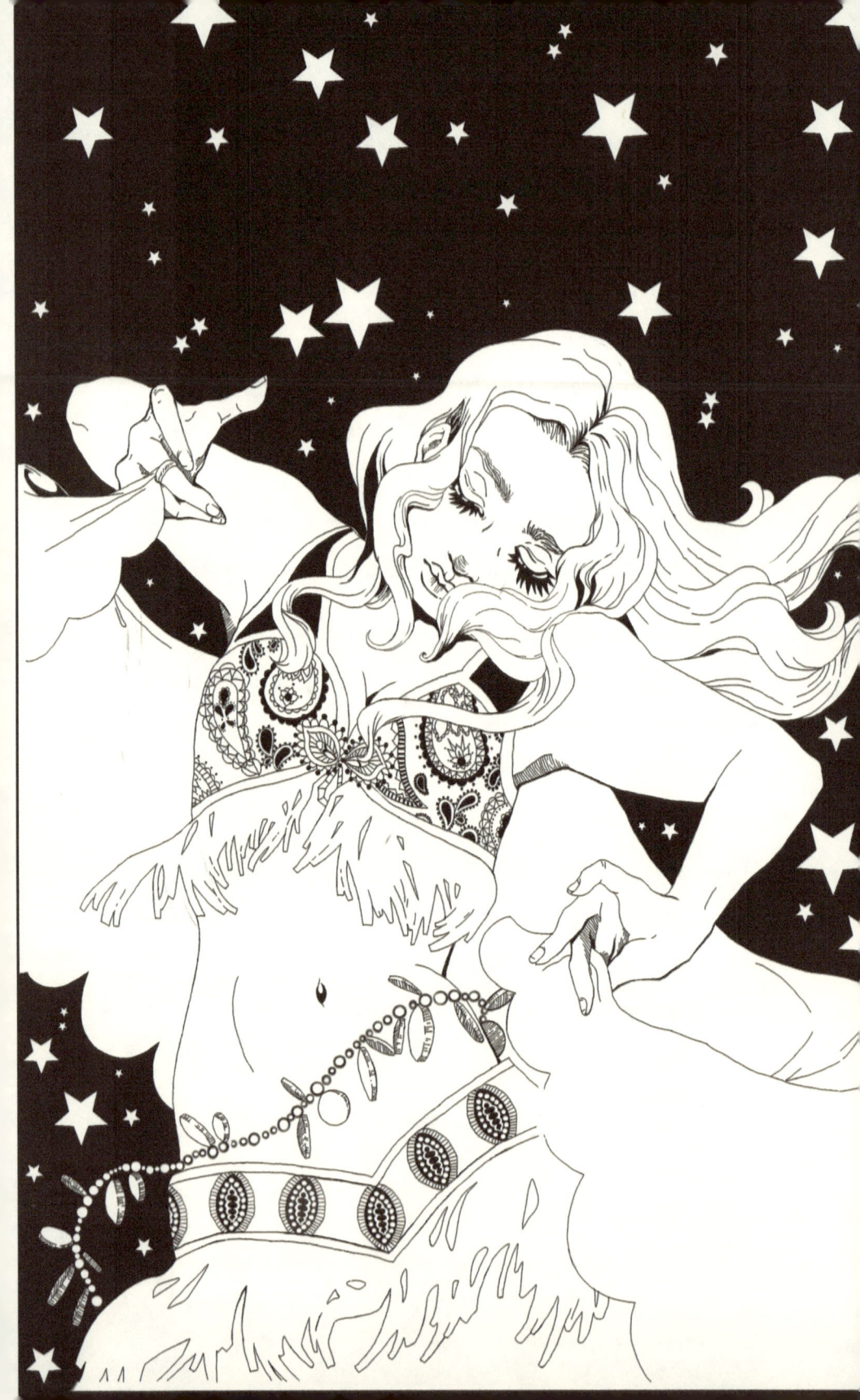

CHAPTER THREE

Money, Money, Money

———————o———————

S omebody is going to be offended by this chapter. I can already picture my stomach flipping as I open an email that is spewing with righteous and indignant comments. How DARE I postulate that ANY dancer perform for BOTH pleasure and gain?! Don't I understand that if you aren't getting paid it doesn't matter? Do I not comprehend that the love of the dance is a reward unto itself? The absolute NERVE!

You can write me if you really want to but my objective will not faulter. It took me, and many of my cohorts, many years to understand what seems like a simple if not decadently blissful truth; you can have your cake and eat it too.

You CAN be paid and immensely enjoy the performance. You CAN be recognized for traditional dances that stretch back a few millenia. You CAN be experimental and still seek a stage and compensation. The pervasive tendency to think that it has to be one or the other and we are all going to fight about it is archaic and needs to go the way of the DoDo. There is absolutely no reason in the modern age that you cannot enjoy what you are doing AND be compensated for it. There, I said it.

I hear your thoughts already. Yes, I would absolutely agree that there are certain types of bellydance styles /music/costuming that are more appropriate (if not required) for certain types of performances. Fusion doesn't usually go over well at multi-cultural festivals and if your booking party has a preference; well you're kind of stuck with it aren't you?

When we think of performing in restuarants we typically think of exuberant cabaret style bellydance with glittery costumes and side slit skirts, zills and happy music. A theatrical showcase is going to arrange it's music, costumes and dance vocabulary to fit the narrative it;s trying to portray to the audience. Multicultural, culturally specific and religious events such as Eid or Nowruz will typically require your perfromance to completely and accurately fit the occasion as well as the nationality of the audience viewing it. These rules are highly unlikely to change anytime soon and dancers attempting to bend them to suit their own fancies have been met with quiet disapproval at best. There is a big difference between the high art of creating the dance of your preference and emotional satisfaction and the enjoyment of presenting what an audience will revel in. Leraning how to appropriately use both at the correct times is one of any artists' biggest lessons.

I'm an Egyptian dancer by trade and by heart, but let me be the first one to tell you that we all have instances where we are asked to do a performance that is out of our comfort zone. I once had a client change their mind and request I use chamber string music for a fancy party...while still bellydancing. I saw a hafla once that was themed around the Chinese New Year. For your convienence I have included the following chart that illustrates what is most likely the appropriate choice when it comes to type of performance:

What music?

Use the following chart as a guideline for choosing what type of music to use in various performance situations. There are exceptions to every rule, and when in doubt ask the event organizer. Always consider the age, cultural background and expectations of your audience.

	Western/American/ Top 40 no remix	Arabic remix versions of songs	Foreign Club & pop music	Mejance/ Classic/ Orchestra	Tribal Fusion/EDM/Trap	Shaabi/ Fokloric/Persian/ Iraq/ etc.
HAFLA & STUDENT SHOW	yes	yes	yes	yes	yes	yes
VARIETY SHOW/ AMERICAN PARTY	maybe	yes/maybe	yes	yes	maybe	yes
FOREIGN PARTY	no	maybe	yes with translations	yes	no	yes with translations
SHOWCASE OR GALA	no	maybe	maybe	yes	yes	yes
MULTICULTURAL FESTIVAL	no	no	yes	yes	no	yes
COMPETITION	no	in the correct category	no	in the correct category	in the correct category	no
RESTAURANT	no	no/maybe	yes	yes	no	yes with translations

However, let's double back and consider that sometimes we WANT to use something different. Some of us aren't inclined towards being strictly traditional at all times and lean more towards fusion or are solely interested in being a hobbyist that picks out music only for the studio hafla. Some of the nastiest fights I have witnessed online (of course) have been over what is appropriate and what is not. Someone usually ends up type-screaming in all caps "IT'S ART AND YOU'RE WRONG! YOU'RE JUST A TRADITIONAL STICK IN THE MUD."

Here's the deal. And again, I know someone will email me but hear me out first.

Both sides are right. Both sides are also wrong.

The issue is not in fact if XYZ performance/style/thing is WRONG or inappropriate, it's whether or not XYZ dance was done in the CORRECT setting or atmosphere for the appropriate clientele. It's whether or not XYZ dance is offensive, well-done and whether we are looking at it from the perspective of personal gain vs. personal pleasure. In short, we should be looking at each dance as it's own entity and assessing it accordingly.

Consider the following rubric for judging performances (including your own): Was the performance in a professional setting? Was it appropriate to the setting it was in? Who was watching it? Are the dancers educated as to what they are doing? Was the performance well executed with appropriate costuming and/or props? Did the performance fit the music? Why was this piece being performed?

Let's take a common example. A student chorepgraphy in which a jazzy top 40 song is chosen to be performed at the student studio hafla.

Was the performance in a professional setting? Clearly not.

Was it appropriate to the setting it was in? Again, clearly not intended to be taken seriously, so yes.

Who was watching it? Friends and family who know it isn't a professional performance and everyone is meant to be having a casually fun time.

Are the dancers educated as to what they are doing? Good question! Let's hope the teacher did let them in on the traditions and differences.

Was the performance well executed with appropriate costuming and/or props? We're going to assume that in this case there were matching belly-casual outfits and everyone looked cute.

Did the performance fit the music? Again, we'll assume it was fun and made to look cute.

Why was this piece being performed? To showcase the students progression and have them enjoy themselves for their families to see.

Let's take another common example. A Middle Eastern dance showcase featuring professional dancers from all over, highlighting bellydance styles from all over the world. We will say this particular performance was from a Tribal Fusion instructor.

Was the performance in a professional setting? Yes, given the acclaim of all the performers.

Was it appropriate to the setting it was in? This could be tricky and it would be prudent to examine the overall theme of the showcase. We'll say in this case it was a variety show and this number was one of many, all of which were different.

Who was watching it? Presumably other dancers and instructors.

Are the dancers educated as to what they are doing? Again, good question! Especially in this setting it's important to know the meaning and intent of both the music and body language.

Was the performance well executed with appropriate costuming and/or props? This is where a trained eye can come in. This particuar setting would call for more than the basics, did the dancer really accomplish what they set out to do? We're going to say since this was an instructor, that the piece was superb in it's execution.

Did the performance fit the music? Again, this setting demands skillful execution and no less than your best.

Why was this piece being performed? As a demonstration of a particular style, a dancers' well known style or to highlight a feature dancer.

Now we can clearly see that comparing these two performances would be like comparing apples to oranges. It would be inappropriate to compare them to each other even if they are both labeled as "fusion" performances. They are of two different calibers, settings, execution and intent. This same logic would apply if we were to compare an Egyptian woman dancing in her own living room with an award winning Modern Oriental professional dancer touring with a production company. They could both be considered "traditional" bellydance but we are clearly speaking of two different types.

Allow me to be clear on one point while we are on the subject. While it would be inappropriate to compare a showcase performance to a restaurant gig to a beginner's student show as I stated, there is never an excuse for sloppiness, poor presentation or just "making it up." If your intention is not clear, with educated movement vocabulary and appropriate accoutrement....well, please spend some more time at the drawing board or in lessons with your teacher. This is where reaching out can be most beneficial. If you are struggling with costuming, meaning or symbolism ask before you take it to the stage. If you are struggling with feeling like you can't accept criticism or advice, please return to page one.

Where does the "gain" part come in?

I happen to be of the opinion that if there is never any sort of financial gain involved, or potentially involved, that students will never escalate their ambitions to the professional level. There are many carrots to chase in this game but actual, honest to goodness pay seems to be one of the few that denotes seriousness and promotes polished performances.

Money conjures up a lot of emotions for people. Feelings of lack and feelings of resentment come up for many people when it comes to entertwining the idea of financial gain with their beloved art forms. For many students accepting money or dancing solely for the intention of being paid (i.e. gigs) makes everything "less fun," or "dirty" in some sort of way. I'll never forget I did a guest feature at a show where a very fresh dancer said to me, "I don't do this to get paid. It's supposed to be fun." And I rebelliously thought, "But getting paid is fun!"

No doubt some of this reaction is due to our ingrained belief that being paid as a dancer is similar to stripping, burlesque, pole dancing and other forms of entertainment that we may have been raised to believe is lewd or beneath us. While Bellydance was, indeed, considered a lewd act itself at one time and was largely a nightclub act in it's early days in America, I happen to be of the belief that the history of the dance is not what is holding back our newer dancers from being paid.

Firstly, the idea of being paid for a gig sounds like a job. It sounds like work and most of us do not equate work with fun. Most of us equate work with doldrum feelings and being told what to do by people who are not working with our best interest in mind. For many students, the idea of being paid to perform drudges up worries of a slimy resturant owner telling them to do what they're told. Sounds downright oppressive to be a professional performer when you think of it that way.

Performing professionally need not be a slave contract or (literally) dancing with the devil. I believe that because Bellydancers are predominantly female and because it is inherently a sensual dance that there is an underlying destructive belief towards apprehension of abusive behavior and selling your body even though there is no sexual exchange whatsoever. Unfortunately this belief is often exacerbated by the public's behavior towards any performer (male or female) that is provacatively costumed and moving sensually. This is the most common fear that has been expressed to me by students who are thinking of gigging; they believe that asking for pay will mean they are "obligated" to endure abusive behavior.

Ask yourself one simple question, "How would I feel if I were paid to perform?" Write your answer here:

If your answer is delighted, excited, or even curious because it hasn't happened yet then you most likely have little to no hang ups understanding that your work deserves an equal exchange of some sort. If you feel pressured, weird, or worried; ask yourself why.

Let's dig deeper. Did you have a bad past experience? Have you witnessed someone having a bad experience? Or maybe it's garden variety nerves that you're now sure how the process goes and are worried that something may go wrong?

What this all generally leads up is confience. Confidence gives us the magic wand that tells us that no matter what happens, we got this under control. Maybe the person who hired you does happen to get weird after you get there. Confidence tells you that you can walk away at any time. Confidence helps you ask the right questions and go to the right people to get answers when you need them. Confidence shows us that even seasoned professional performers sometimes have slip ups and they aren't banished into exile forever by their peers.

Confidence needs back up though. Confidence just doesn't roll in like a cold front in Autumn and annouce itself. It needs a little push from it's more secretive cousin- Competence.

Further thoughts:

The process of booking and interacting with clients to produce paying gigs is typically referred to as "the business of bellydance." What scares you most about this process? Have you felt successful or unsuccessful in the past? What do you feel you need the most help on?

It can be very helpful to have a trusted teacher or mentor to guide you until you feel more secure in the process on your own.

CHAPTER 4

How to Gig It

———————○———————

Confidence is often mistaken for arrogance. Confidence is not walking into a room and expecting everyone to like you. Confidence is walking into the room and being fine if everyone doesn't.

In this chapter we are going to delve into the business side of things. Regrettably this portion can date itself very quickly since marketing tactics, pay rates, and technology change very rapidly and affect the entertainment industry constantly. However, I'll be covering an easy checklist to keep in mind when approaching or being approached by potential clients as well as advice that never goes out of style.

A. Manifest it!

It's going to sound counter-intuitive at first but you actually want to prepare for success before you get it. Read that again.

So many people get caught off guard with a potential client calling or asking them to perform that this preparation deserves special attention. When you decide that you want to start performing, begin to think about what that will entail before an actual booking takes place. What kind of costumes will you need? Makeup? Could you put together a full set if necessary? Let's break it down.

Let's begin with costumes since that is typically the most expensive initial investment of a performer outside of lessons. You need at least two to really get the ball rolling. I always advise any bellydancer starting out to invest in a metallic colored sequin bedlah set (the two piece bra and belt). Gold or SIlver will match anything and with proper care the set will last many years. It can be matched with numerous types of skirts or pants, accessories, boleros and used in any dance situation you can think of. Some dancers buy one in both colors for nearly endless mix and match opportunities.

Your second costume is a little more to your preference and what you believe will most likely be the direction your dance will be going. If you are going to the private gig/restuarant/ corporate side of things you'll most likely want to have a two piece cabaret costume or baladi dress. Think dressy and elegant with lots of sparkle! If you are most likely going towards theatrical showcases or tribal style your second costume will most likely be determined by your director or troupe leader. It's not a bad idea to begin to look for pieces to make or buy that will be able to mix and match.

If you're crafty there are many used costumes floating around out there that can be altered and redecorated or even patterns to download and make costumes from scratch. Buying used costumes in general really helps save money and gives you an idea of what to look for as you start wearing more costumes. Think about what type of regular clothing you tend to favor and start there. Great costume choices are not just "what's in style" or what looks expensive. They should be comfortable, flattering and easy to put on and take off. If you are self conscious about certain parts of your body (which is understandable and by no means a mark against you) start looking for costumes that creatively work around those areas or other solutions such as stomach covers or mesh sleeves. Love the costume but not sure about what color to pick? Head to the paint department in your local hardware store and find a free paint color chip to take home and look at in different lighting against your skin.

Filtering through costumes online can be a bit overwhelming and feel crazy given that we don't normally choose clothes that look that revealing or extravagant. I always say, err on the side of feeling comfortable. When you feel comfortable, it will show in your dance and both you and the viewer will enjoy it more. Alternatively, choose something that you know you can alter easily such as adding sleeves or more jewels.

The next step is music. Ask your teachers and friends for help with finding music that will suit what you'd like to do. Start identifying where there might be gaps in your music knowledge. Every dancer, regardless of style, should keep a set ready on their music player for a 20-25 minute set. Have it ready to go at a moment's notice! I always tell my students no matter what style they choose to go towards that they should know at least one classic song (Alf Leyla, Zeina, etc), one drum solo, and at least one Taqsim or instrumental piece.

A good set to keep on hand is exciting, fun, has variety and can be used with or without props. Traditionally speaking, a Cabaret set had five parts and in America could be a mix of harmonious songs ranging from Egyptian to Turkish.

I am of the personal opinion that your set will be easier to perfrom to and digest for the audience if you stick with a general theme, I.E. all Egyptian or all vintage, etc. Most dancers will have several sets planned out for that reason. I have several themed playlists on my iPod such as Greek music, upbeat music, Persian, Turkish, Halloween music, Vintage and more for easy set building purposes.

Piper Reid Hunt described in her article in the Gilded Serpent that the generic 5-part routine included:

1. A fast exciting entrance piece
2. a slower piece for veil work
3. An up tempo number to get people clapping
4. A slow piece for floor work, sword balancing, etc
5. Drum solo plus finale.

I'd like to add several points to this. Firstly let's note that the basic structure of this plan is fast, slow, fast, slow, fast. This has a couple of purposes. Namely, it gives the dancer some breathing time. However, even if you can go fast through the whole set and have great stamina; variety in timing and instrumentation allows for more variety in your movement which ultimately creates more interest. Audiences really don't mind some slower music and the contrast will help your drum solos and exciting fast moves stick out more. It furthermore showcases your expertise as a dancer.

Let's call attention to a few snafus you might experience.

Firstly, not every gig will require a full twenty minutes, or may ask for more. You may need to adjust the time so keeping a full music library will make your life easier. Being familiar with basic sound editing software or having a trusty audio expert friend on stand by will serve you well. (Also consider if your pricing will change depending on if you need to shorten or lengthen a set. Thinking ahead on this one will save you some awkward pauses while you're on the phone with someone.)

Secondly, don't make the mistake of making your set absolutely contingent on specific props. We'd all love to open our carefully planned routines with giant isis wings and incorporate dramatic sword pieces with impressive floor work. Unfortunately you are at the mercy of the venue here. You may not have enough space, high enough ceilings or room in between patron seating to pull off specific props safely. Veils and fan veils are always good choices because they are not hard and will not hurt if they touch a patron. They can substitute for isis wings in a pinch. It's happened to me more than once that I was saved by keeping a spare veil in my bag because I wasn't accurately told how small of a space I'd be dancing in!

However, and this is a big however, be prepared to execute the set with no props at all. Never, ever forget that you are a dancer and not just a decorated prop holder. Props are fun, impressive and add variety; but you are ultimately the show.

Lastly, start thinking about footwear.

Wait, what?

No, I'm serious. This is a big one I wish someone had told me when I started performing so I'm sparing you the shock of arriving at a venue and realizing you may hurt yourself dancing barefoot. As students we tend to be spoiled with dancing barefooted in our clean studios and get very used to feeling the floor under our feet with natural traction. Now picture this: you're in a restaurant or bar where small children have thrown their food on the floor, patrons have tracked in mud from the rain outside and a waiter has dropped a glass and quickly swept up the majority without checking for small splinters. Maybe you've arrived at a charity benefit where the social elite are stuffing white envelopes with hundreds of dollars wearing black tie attire. Your dance area is carpeted. Or outside. Or concrete. The list goes on. Leather sandals once saved me from having a beer bottle cap in my foot while dancing in a dark resturant. I danced the whole set with it stuck in the bottom sole! It was so heavily embedded that I had to throw the pair out.

This is such a strange topic in the bellydance world because no one talks about it until you start performing professionally. In every other type of dance, there are specific shoes that you wear and you begin wearing them in the studio on day one. There are even tiny ballet slippers for toddlers. I'm not exactly sure how we indefinitely have chosen to miss the boat but there are numerous articles describing the process of how bellydancers lost their shoes. Samia Gamal is widely credited with starting the trend in the 1940s when she broke a shoe during a set in a nightclub and became the first dancer to kick them off and keep dancing. The story goes the crowd went wild and other dancers followed suit to capitalize on the craze.

Look for a shoe that bends in the arch with a leather-soled bottom. Leather ballet slippers, low heeled salsa or ballroom shoes, "hermes" sandals, jazz shoes and even Irish Ghillies are popular choices. A good guide is to match the formality of the shoe to the event (ballroom shoes at a wedding for example) and remember that the softer the shoe the more likely it will tear on rough surfaces. Clients tend not to think that their outside deck or concrete backyard will be an issue because they do not dance on it. Not all stages are in great repair, either. Protecting your feet is the ultimate investment and will be well worth it when you avoid injury! As far as dancing in them? Practice, practice, practice. Take them to the studio and ask your teacher if you can wear them in class. Walk around the house in them. Practice your routines in them. And absolutely check them over and try them on one more time before you leave the house to go perform.

Seems like quite a bit before you even get a booking, right? Trust me when I say setting yourself up and being ready for the booking to come will help you avoid a lot of last minute panicking and potential mistake making. It will also serve the very important purpose of giving you the confidence to immediately say "Yes!" when you are approached instead of hesitating because you aren't sure how you'll pull it off. Setting yourself up for success is a beautiful thing and will teach you so much during the process.

B. Getting the booking

Man, oh man. This has got to THE topic most budding dancers ask about.

This is where all of that prep work comes into play (or maybe it doesn't if you've been contacted before you even got a chance to think about it!) and now you can start to assemble your performance to deliver to the client.

Bookings typically happen in one of two ways. You approach the venue or client and they then hire you. Or, the client approaches you and you agree to the booking. Sounds simple, right? The reality is this has more to do with marketing than anything else. This is truly what they mean whan they say, "The Business of Bellydance." It's time to start thinking of yourself as both a business entity and a sellable product. Just like any other type of service you must be able to describe yourself, market yourself, get found by your potential customer and be competitive in your pricing without undermining the cost of your supplies and time.

That sounds terrifying! And complicated! And if you wanted to do that you'd open a corner store! It's not as crazy as it sounds if you can navigate yourself appropriately and most importantly ask questions along the way.

Step 1: Marketing

Demographic is a more specific marketing term that means the people you want to sell a good or service to. Most dancers make the mistake of thinking that they should market to as many people as possible and literally anyone could be a customer. While random bookings from unexpected places do happen, the majority of your clientele will most likely be more specific than you realize due to location, affliations, age group and economic status.

The same applies if you are advertising for classes or even pitching a student showcase. Every facet of what you may want to do will have a different target audience and your presentation on your website, social media and business materials such as cards should reflect that.

Let's stick with the example of solely advertising for gig bookings. It's not hard to imagine that advertising in a low income area with flashy materials probably won't work out well. A little research online is prudent in this case. Looking up the average income, home value and generally determining the "vibe" of your local area will give you a lot of insight.

Is your city rustic? Metropolitan? What kind of cars do the wealthy drive? The non wealthy? Where do they live? Why did they choose that area? Do you have a bustling historic district or is your downtown stretched with looming sleek modern buildings? When you look at the signs and printed material of successful restaurants and businesses in your area, what fonts and colors do they use? Do they attract the age and type of people that may hire you? Now more importantly, what types of entertainment tend to do well in your area? What was the most popular concert that came through your city recently? Sometimes on artist's websites you can request a press kit or media kit that will contain all kinds of printed material. Otherwise, check out their social media and see how they use design to get their message across.

There is a huge amount of psychology that large companies pay big bucks for research on when it comes to colors and fonts used in marketing material. In general, warm colors are "invigorating" and "exciting" while cool colors are "calming" and "trainquil" with many variations in-between. Dark colors tend to express either somber themes or very expensive product (high end luxury cars for example) and light colors or pastels are used for more wistful endeavors such as spas or meditation classes.

When it comes to fonts, the worst mistake I see over and over again is the use of such loopy curvy fonts that the message is lost simply because it is illegible. Especially if you have an uncommon or foreign-sounding name, please do yourself a favor and use a font that is still easy to read while fulfilling the purpose you desire. This does not mean everything must be in Times New Roman; but it does mean you need to experiment a little and do your research. Colors are a little obvious but few of us understand the subtle psychological effects of font in marketing. It is well worth the research! Take a gander on your next car ride and you will see signs printed in every type imaginable and notice what was chosen for each business.

The Very Basics of Font

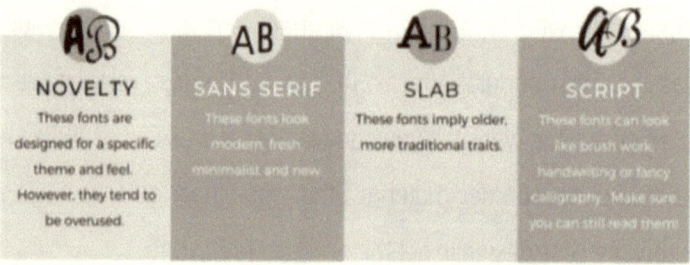

NOVELTY	SANS SERIF	SLAB	SCRIPT
These fonts are designed for a specific theme and feel. However, they tend to be overused.	These fonts look modern, fresh, minimalist and new.	These fonts imply older, more traditional traits.	These fonts can look like brush work, handwriting or fancy calligraphy. Make sure you can still read them!

It's not a bad idea to check out other belly dancer's websites and social media in your area. Try not to look at them from a place of self-comparison but rather from a customer's standpoint. Please avoid copying from the other dancers, but it's worth it to peek at someone that you feel is on the same level as you professionally, above you and below you.

Even if you consider yourself a demi or semi-professional dancer it's worth it to at least set up a Facebook Fan Page (or "Like" Page) to direct potential bookings and/or students to. Professionals should absolutely have a regular website and a Facebook page, along with other social media. The number one thing clients look for whether they are requesting entertainment or instruction is proof that you do what you say you do.

You can include all the fancy little knicknack graphics and fonts that you want but current photos and videos are the meat and potatoes that will seal the deal.

When I was first developing my website (I was on a budget so I did everything myself), I would have my non-dancer friends look at it and give me their feedback. This is very important: get some non dancer eyes on everything that you create to market with. We as bellydancers seem to think that everything we do must be laden with rhinestones, glitter, ultra loopy fonts, henna designs, complicated page transitions, and music playing in the background like an old MySpace page. I've seen this done well but I've also seen websites where I literally had no idea what was going on with it. I couldn't even find an email address to contact the person.

My good friend who had done graphic work herself for years gave me some incredible advice when it came to websites and marketing in general, "All people care about is seeing what you do, if you look good doing it, and how much you cost." I have stuck by these guidelines ever since.

Also take into consideration this gem of wisdom: If a client cannot find the information they are looking for within three clicks, they lose interest and you have lost the sale. Obviously this is especially true if you are selling an actual product like costumes, accessories, music or even listing workshops. Make it easy for anyone looking you up, whether it's on Facebook or a website, to see what you do, how good you look doing it, how much you cost and how to contact you. Everything after that is dealer's choice. Don't let it overwhelm you, you can always change something you don't like!

If the idea of making your own graphics and website, or even FB page gives you heart plapitations enlist the help of a trusted friend or graphic designer. There are many dancers out there who moonlight as designers that offer their services, plus they'll know just what you want! If you go this route, understand that artists need to be compensated for their services but the results will be worth it.

Step 2: Hook Em

Ok so you have your website, facebook, music and costumes at the ready. And....here we sit. Why is no one booking you?

Have you ever gotten a job solely by wishful thinking?

There are several ways to start directing eyes to you (this is called traffic conversion in marketing land). Firstly, take your FB page and ask your esteemed friends, family, and students to kindly give you a "like" and share it. Then, make sure ALL of yorur social media stays active! Post about your classes, what you're up to in dance, videos, photos, etc. Ask your buddies to like and share those too until you gain some momentum. The worst thing you could do is NOTHING, so don't let your pages just sit there collecting moths! You want to look like you are prolific, not just busy. Busy has become the new "thing." So much of social media has become a highlight reel of people's fantasy lives that it can feel like you have to be on yoru phone 24/7. Not true. In fact, this is counter productive. People who actually know you in your local area will know that you do not own a yacht and haven't taken a vacation past your driveway in years. Post real posts. And, please, stop posting your dinner unless you are writing for a food magazine.

Pro tip: There are several free apps for your phone that can schedule posts, create posts and posts for you. Work smarter, not harder. I even know of a few who bribe younger siblings or nephews to post for them. If you aren't social media savvy, you better learn or be prepared to pay someone who is. There is simply no getting around this iceburg.

Secondly, take that website you made and link it to EVERYTHING. Put it on your cards, your FB info, in your statuses, paper flyers, etc. Now take that website and all of the info in it and list yourself on websites that are pertinent to what you want to do. There are tons of gig booking agency websites, event listings, local newsletters and free publications that you can submit information to.

Thirdly, start talking to people. Hand your information out. If someone contacts you online (or you reach out to them), send them your website to prove you can back up what you're saying to them. Sending your website (or FB page) is also a great way to "warm up" a client so that you ultimately end up answering less trivial questions and get more quickly to the point of them saying "YES."

If this sounds like salesmenship tactics, it is. There is to difference between selling a TV and selling a costume. Or, selling someone on taking classes with you versus the local gym. No amount of glitter changes the fact that we are in sales. It doesn't mean you have to be slimey, or coercive, or even pushy. All of the time spent on gathering the right materials and building the right website serves to provide the proof your clients need that you are what they are looking for so that you are off the hook when it comes to convincing. The right marketing materials do most of the talking for you.

Notice I said MOST. Sorry to inform you but you will need to speak to clients, students, agents and someone even just curious passers by. I know this is the part most people dread. Even after all my years of professional performing, I still get a little nervous when I have to speak with a client I've never known before on the phone. Are they going to be rude? Will they argue my pricing? Have they bothered to look at my website first before calling? Have they spoken to other dancers before calling me? Eek. Take a deep breath, listen acitively and take it one step at a time.

Worksheet:

Take a look at another local dancer's website, and at a dancer's site that is not near you (out of town or out of country, or both!)

A. What do you notice first about each website?

B. How would you describe the fonts?

C. Can you find information easily?

D. Do they seem proficient and a good choice for performances and/or classes?

E. What kind of "vibe" are you getting? Why?

F. How about colors? Warm or cool? How do they make you feel?

&. For my website or graphic images I am thinking of using:

colors:

fonts:

photos:

Stage Fright and Public Speaking for Dancers

It's embarassing for most dancers who have stage fright or a fear of speaking to admit to that they do. It's also hard for others to understand when someone can get up on stage for a living and totally choke on the phone or struggle to teach a workshop. Even worse, taking years of instruction and completely freezing up when the opportunity presents itself to perform for fear of the worst case scenario.

All of these scenarios lead to the same problem many, many people face in their daily lives whether it's in a boardroom or on a playing field: Fear of Failure.

By now all of us have seen enough motivational posters and internet memes about "just taking the first step" or "beginning the journey" but what does that even mean? As dancers, we sometimes have a selective fear that isn't really discussed often. We can get up on stage and pour our hearts out nonverbally and then struggle to call the pizza guy. Or, conversely, be an ace at teaching and taking group choreography and then convienently be always "busy" when it comes time to perform a solo.

I've heard several equally valid reasons from my students over the years ranging from being naturally introverted, to mental illness, to being a perfectionist, to even being afraid they would disappoint me as a teacher.

Here are a couple of tools I've learned as a Confidence Coach that really help performers with both stage fright and public speaking:

1. Develop an alter ego.

I'm dead serious because I used this one myself. A method used by actors and business professionals alike; imagining yourself as another person takes the pressure off the situation because it's not happening to "you." It also gives you guidelines when it comes to responses, behaviors and choices.

When I first started dancing I was very self-conscious and rather shy. You wouldn't guess that to know me now but I needed a little help when it came to putting myself out there. I also had short hair at the time, being fresh from working at a doctor's office. I created the character of "Oriana" by combining my biggest inspirations at the time: Greta Garbo the 1930's silent film actress, Rita Hayworth the 1940's film actress, and Jillina (the only other red-headed bellydancer I knew at the time).

I'm not sure if I ever officially wrote it down, but "Oriana" became a young girl from the 1930's from an affluent family who grew too curious for her own good and ran away to join the circus. It might sound downright silly but this simple narrative allowed me the freedom to style my hair as I could (short hair was popular in the 1930's), follow cues on my stage presence (if you need ideas on how to nonverbally express yourself, the silent films are no shortage of inspiration), and even formulate how to respond to awkward situations (the daughter of a wealthy baron would NEVER allow herself to be treated poorly! How DARE you).

Eventually I didn't need to adhere to this story as I gained more confidence and found my own voice as a performer. However, if you know me, some remnants remain and I still fondly recall the films I watched to help me choreograph my first solos.

Even if you feel you don't need an elaborate back story, it's not only fun but helpful to reimagine yourself as your performer persona. Think of it as roleplaying or even an extension of acting and watch your acts develop new depth. Anyone with theater experience will tell you that it is much easier to express difficult, silly or even embarassing emotions on stage when you feel like the audience isn't watching YOU.

My Alter Ego

1. If I could have been born in any time period I wish it was_____

2. My favorite fashion style is _____

3. My favorite colors are _____

4. The characters I most admire in fiction are _____

5. If I were a character in a movie I'd be_____

6. When I think of the style of bellydance I love, I think of these traits (dark, light, majestic, fluid, etc) _____

7. My own real interests outside of bellydance are _____

8. My alter ego's name is:

She/He/They were born:

Their family is:

They enjoy:

Their style is:

Their idea of fun is:

Their values are:

Their goals are:

2. Visualization and Anchor Points

This one combines an oldie (but a goodie) with some psychology. This is useful in any situation that requires memorization but here we'll use it for those who often feel "like I get on stage and instantly forget everything I was going to do!"

The first is Visualization. When you are practicing your number, every odd practice or so, sit down and see it in your mind's eye instead of going through the motions physically. Go a little deeper. Change the movements in your head if needed and even visualize yourself on a stage using emotion and seeing the audience's reaction. With a little more effort and practice you can even change your feeling towards it to be like that of a memory. It already happened! Let go and feel grateful for a job well done and a successful performance already under your belt. Imagining the stress of the situation as in the past tells your protective brain that there is nothing to worry about completing the action in the future because you've already done it successfully.

I like to combine this with a technique developed in the 1970s called Anchor Points, or simply Anchoring, in the Neuro- Linguistic Programming field. Choose an easily accessible part of your body that you can apply pressure to. Most people tend to choose a fingr to pull, the pulse point of the wrist, the earlobe or the skin between the thumb and index finger. The choice is enturely yours so long as you can remember it and discreetly locate it when needed. The great thing about this technique is that it can used for virtually any situation; from going to stage to a case of the nerves before teaching.

Next, imagine the happiest memory that you can muster. Let it fill you up until you are brimming with joy and happiness while recalling every detail as vividly as you possibly can. When you are at the height of the emotion, squeeze or apply pressure to your chosen anchor point.

Then, imagine your desired outcome. Let's say receiving a standing ovation on stage after executing a killer performance. Let the feeling of praise, admiration and success completely overwhelm you as you bask in the glory of your hard work. Or, you're confidently and deftly teaching your first workshop with perfection. Your students are eating it up and asking for more! Touch your anchor point.

Repeat this process when you have a few quiet moments for at least a week. Then, repeat it in environments when you are potentially distracted like in a resturant or walking down the street. Finally, when you are in the actual moment and feeling the undesired emotion of panic- hit your trigger point. You will have conditioned your mind to associate this action with the desired response (joy and confidence) and your fear will wash away.

3. The Najmah Technique

I have named this one after one of my teachers, Najmah Nour. I learned this from her and I share it with you now because it has formulated my confidence immensely in dance.

Najmah taught us a lot of improv but she did so in a unique way. She would come around to each of us and whisper a word in our ears. They were abstract concepts like "blue," "sun," "flying," etc. She would then put on a random piece of music and our challenge was to enact our interpretation of the concept we were given while still honoring the tempo and motifs we heard in the music. It sounds complicated, but it's actually very simple and produces stunning results while injecting that extra layer of soul into it.

Let's say the music your are choregraphing sounds joyful and happy to you. Assign the word "waves" to it and watch how your mind automatically might conjure up undulations, level changes, snake arms, etc. Now you've been given moves you might have been drawing a blank on and a possible narrative.

This is a great technique to also get you "in the mood" when you are about to go on stage. Especially if you are attempting an emotionally difficult piece. It is far easier to focus on one word than an entire story.

Learn To Say YES and NO

Most performers' trepidation regarding getting that email or phone call is that there are ulterior motives involved. "What if?" begins to cloud the mind and many female performers especially are afraid to accept private gigs by themselves or even at all.

All performers fear getting the request from someone who is unorganized, difficult to work with, nefarious or just downright ridiculous. For some this fear of what could happen overtakes the love of performing so much that they are too anxious to step past student shows into paying work.

It is truly understandable. A brief peek at the news reels will make you not want to leave the house! Unfortunately it's not all theatrics either, bad things can and do happen and people wanting to take advantage of a dancer is not exception. It is absolutely always better to err on the side of caution than be taken by surprise.

However, keeping that in mind, there is no reason fear should hold you back from being financially successful in your craft. Whether you are being approached or are the one doing the approaching, there are ways to protect yourself while still answering when opportunity knocks.

First of all, setting the tone will eliminate a vast majority of issues before they even occur. Answer the phone professionally, not casually, and refrain from being flirtatious or too familiar. If you are meeting in person dress like you are going to a job interview. Have your press kit or proposal typed and in a folder ready to present. Have business cards at the ready. Cracking a few jokes or getting to know each other is fine, but stay on track with the business at hand.

Make a working list of things you know you'd be ok with or want, things you will never be ok with and things that might be negotiable. These lists will change over time. Know your price and stick with it. This can be especially hard when it feels like you haven't gotten work in ages. A very wise female entrepreneur friend of mine once told me, "Hold the line. If they want what you have, they'll pay." I argued in my mind if that applied to entertainment until I realized what she was really alluding to was quality over quantity. One real, paying, supportive and legit customer is better than ten sloppy, cheap and frivolous gigs.

It sounds like common sense or even a little old fashioned; but I place so much importance on these initial tactics because first impressions really are everything. You want to set the tone as a professional artist. You cannot be deceived, deterred, distracted or dumbfounded. You may lose a few people in this approach but you can be assured they probably weren't that serious about you as an artist. The idea is that you want to look like a lion, not a tiny kitten. The opportunist who wants to get their giggles in by hiring a bellydancer to treat poorly will not mess with an artist who has all their ducks in a row and comes in overwhelmingly projecting professionalism. This isn't to say that you need to walk in with your chaps and gun holster playing hardball and overanalyzing the conversation. On the contrary, be as cool as a cucumber. A cucumber with the ace up their sleeve- the ability to be confident in the situation because you already know what you want and won't settle for less.

As I said, this deters the opportunist. There are still some really disorganized and flippant clients floating around. A Performer's Contract can be a useful tool to make sure everything is clear before a project begins or when planning a gig in advance. This is also the reason I insist on an email or written confirmation of a booking. Having a contract will not necessarily gaurantee you anything in a court of law, but it will back you up in the event someone goes back on their word or something is forgotten.

Finally, and it almost goes without saying, if something does not feel right to you- you're probably right. You do not owe anyone an explanation on why you feel uneasy or have backed out of a gig. Yes, some people may still judge you or be mad with you. Let them stew. I know it's easier said than done but your intuition is your greatest defense against something going awry. We all have an inner guide that alerts us when we see something in person or in writing that just doesn't seem kosher, even if we can't explain why. Listen to it, have a friend look at it, but don't ignore it. Learn to trust this voice and you will pick up on things that others seem to miss.

It's ok to say NO. It is equally ok to say YES in faith that you can handle whatever gets thrown at you. All else fails, I use a little something that same female entrepreneur taught me; what she affectionately called an "Asshole Tax." She turned to me and said if someone was giving her or her staff issues that they would suddenly find themselves unable to afford the service. A surefire way to get someone off your back if it seems suspicious is to blow smoke their way with an exorbatant price. You can also view it not just as a gate keeping method but also a payment for your on sanity. If someone has been particulary annoying you aren't out of bounds to ask that they reimburse you for wasting your precious time. They'll back off really quickly.

It is absolutely possible to be a joy to work with and not bend over backwards or over step your personal boundaries. You want to be hired and sought after for being an amazing artist that is pleasant and easy to work with. Say please and thank you. Respond promptly. Respect deadlines. Fill out the forms. Answer questions and provide feedback. Actively listen. Be on time. Be ready.

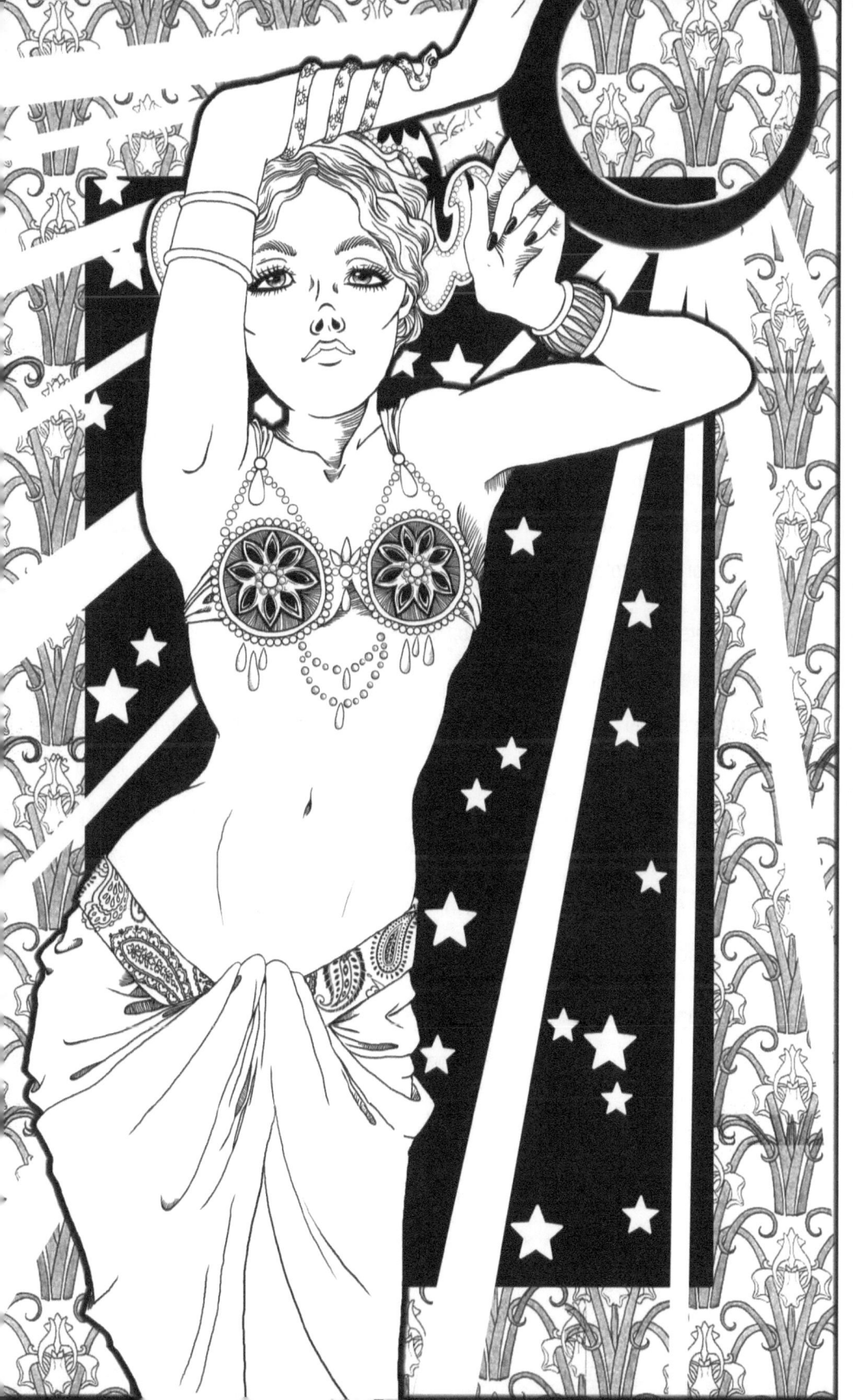

CHAPTER 5

Hey, Teach!

Teaching is an art, science and skillset all to its own. It is seperate from being an excellent performer, yet benefits from it. The skills and practice required to master the dance are vital to being able to teach it but it's only one piece of the whole pie.

Lets get one thing out in the open right away: not everyone is cut out to be a teacher. Being a professional performer, choreographer, director or even just having studied for X amount of years is not an automatic green great that you will be a good teacher. Teaching dance classes isn't something you should just take on because you're trying to get your name out or advance your reputation either. This is a topic I've seen many fights break out over as studio owners push their students to accept teaching positions or performers feel they need extra income.

Being its own profession, teaching is something that is often quoted as something that should be done "from the heart." But what does that actually mean? Most people are under the impression that teaching requires infinite and inhuman amounts of patience and a sublime ability to handle everything with kid gloves and gentle words. Having patience certainly helps but it is merely a symptom of the larger portion that all teachers must have to be great: unwaivering passion for what they teach.

Teachers are in purpetual service. They are in service to their students first and foremost and then in service to the greater cloud of knowledge and community which they represent. Teaching requires empathy, intuition and a commitment to serving the needs of those asking for your guidance. In the age of social media it also means receiving messages at all hours, video calls, emails and hunting down obscure music tracks at 2 am.

Yes, there is some hand holding. However, great teachers intuitively step into their student's shoes perceive the needs of their students. We are not here to baby adult students and cater to their whims. But we are here when emotions come up during challenging choreography ready with words of encouragement and the tools to help them push through. You are not a parent, you are a counselor. You are not a babysitter. You are a guide.

Think back to your school days. Sure they were probably not dance classes but I can gaurantee you had teachers that you loved and teachers that you hated. Why did you love the ones that you did? Why did you dread History with Mr. Smith in 10th grade even though you later realized you liked history? I'm willing to put some money down that it had to do with their demeanor, speech and inflection towards the class.

You may be at this point in the chapter and be saying "Maybe I should skip this, I don't want to teach." This part still applies to you as a student, a studio owner, a friend of a studio owner, an assistant, a stage manager, a workshop attendee, etc etc. And by the way, may I add here that reading a bunch of self help books like this one and spiritual methods does not automatically make you above average. I have known quite a few studio owners my time that did not practice what they preached and had a gazillion yoga certification hours or did A Course in Miracle like 20 times. I worked for one guy that would continually bark at us in what seemed like the most tense team meetings ever about getting out of our "poverty mindsets" and our "limiting beliefs" only to turn around and whine about why he was the only one doing any work around here and no one helps him and he's so alone. Very spiritual of him. It wasn't that surprising that his business was tanking and the staff kept rotating, despite having crystal grids and Buddhas in every corner.

I promise this will still benefit you. The only thing better than knowing how to be a good teacher is knowing how to spot one.

A great teacher:

- Should be kind, use appropriate wording and be easy to understand

- should present the material in plain language before using fancy terms

- should always be on time

- should be equally talking and listening by posing questions to the class

-should say far more positive things than negative ("Great job!" " Try it again, you're almost there!" "Let's try that two more times, ok?" as opposed to "That's all wrong. " "You look silly" or "Why aren't you getting it?")

-Is not a beginner in their field and has mastery of all aspects of what they are teaching.

- should NEVER body shame. I'm embarrased to say I've heard teachers tell students that they cannot do certain moves such as flutters because of their body type. Learned and experienced professionals know this is simply untrue.

- does not discuss hot topics in the classroom (politics, religion outside of what pertains to the studies in class, news reports etc).

- is willing to talk before and after class to answer questions

-can adapt the material to suit injuries, disabilities and different styles.

- passes on opportunities to their students, even if it's outside of the studio.

- takes time to research the material and choose appropriate music and choreography to present.

and most importantly:

Is a lifelong student themselves.

If you really, really love this dance you won't want to stop learning it yourself even if you've begun teaching (or are thinking about it). I think maybe we get it stuck in our heads that being a teacher means being the guru at the top of the mountain; we are expected to "know it all" and "have all the answers" so we think that continuing to take classes makes us look bad. We don't know it all and therefore shouldn't be teaching.

Doesn't that sound silly when you read it on paper?

We stop learning when we are placed in our eternal rest in Mother Earth. Simple as that. Continuing to train, attend workshops or even still take weekly classes is a sign of someone who is committed; not someone who is not worthy of instructing. In fact, my personal opinion is that it's a bad sign if someone who never continues their education at all. Even the elders among us who have been dancing 20, 30, 40 years plus have sat in symposiums and traded notes with their peers. The corporate, scientific, hostorical etc etc etc professionals all have continuing education in their fields and some, like massage therapy, even require it! The idea is to keep your knowledge fresh and razor sharp. This is something I throughly believe we should adopt more readily in the bellydance community. If you're concerned your students will look down on you, don't be. I've found just the opposite. Students have more respect for those who are active in their field. Point blank.

Teaching doesn't mean you have all the answers. Not having all the answers doesn't mean you shouldn't teach. The difference lies in being committed to always pursuing knowledge and pushing yourself to be a better dancer and educator. If you don't know answer, promise that you will find out. And then go find out. That is why teaching is it's own special field.

You should feel a call to teach. Some people describe it as a longing to pass down their information. Some people feel like they are bursting at the seams and have to get the knowledge out there or they are going to lose their minds. Still others feel peace and completely natural with exchanging ideas and presenting material to others.

Conversely what happens if you've been asked to teach and you're not sure you're ready? Or maybe it's been suggested that you teach because you have so much to share but you feel doubtful of your abilities or even self conscious?

My Favorite Teacher Worksheet

What was your favorite subhect in school?

Who was your favorite teacher of all time?

What dance workshop did you enjoy the most? Why?

Who is your favorite dance teacher? Why?

The thing that scares me most about teaching is:

The thing that excites me most about teaching is:

The subject I feel most knowledgeable about is:

The subject I feel least knowledgeable about is:

My favorite studio is:

My ideal studio space would be:

There are many ways for beginners and established teachers alike to share their knowledge and technology is making advances everyday to aid the experience.

Personally, I think the worst mistake for beginning teachers is to be saddled with a class inside a studio where the expectation is that they help support or increase the class sizes and make the studio lots of money. If you're just starting out you may not feel that you have enough material to even warrant a weekly class.

A great solution is to offer a workshop instead. It allows you a test run to see if you want to teach, like the studio, feel that there is enough interest there and in turn let's the studio owner know that you're willing to compromise. You can even pitch it as a type of audition if you like (angle it so it seems that it's to the studio owner's benefit to test you out as well).

More solutions include video classes or live streaming classes. This path has the added bonus of creating some physical distance from your students if you suffer from a fear of public speaking. The downside, of course, to virtual classes is just that- the lack of physical connection. For beginner levels especially it can be difficult to follow along and execute movements correctly without a live teacher to correct them in a classroom setting. However, for the beginning teacher it's great practice inlearning how to organize your thoughts and materials, demonstrate the movements and get into the flow of conducting a classroom structure. Plus, you can always use the archived videos to send into studio owners as evidence of your teaching ability. Filmed yourself and still not feeling great about it? No harm done- just delete it.

You can also simply coach or mentor exclusively on one topic you know very well to get started. Examples may include competing, sewing, or even stage makeup- anything you know from the inside out.

As I mentioned before, the expectation that we will be questioned and found lacking prevents many worthy potential teachers from getting their feet wet and starting to mentor others. The reality is that so many feel uncompetent in their abilities or lack resources to coss refrenc in the classroom. Or both. And while we're being honest, a lot of our local dance communities are not doling out compliments on a regular basis. Bullying creates a perpetual cycle that damages communities from the inside out. There are few things more tragic in my opinion than when a teacher detroys a student's self esteem. Sometimes it's unintentional, but always preventable.

I'm willing to bet really good money that if you're feeling the jitters or are actively avoiding teaching out of fear; somewhere in your backstory of what may seem like solely doubting our own knowledge there is a former teacher, mentor or even a parental figure that was a meanie. Maybe you kept getting turned down for shows or even worse you were blatantly discriminated against. Maybe you were deterred from advancing. Maybe you had a nasty blowout and your trust was irrevocably broken.

Teacher and student relationships remind me so much of romantic relationships sometimes it's dizzying. Years of effort and friendship can be shattered instantly over one show, ill timed mistake or the poor intent of one person in the party. And hurtful words can last a lifetime.

It's important to understand before you begin teaching that you too might make some mistakes with students. However, it's prudent and most beneficial if we can wipe the slate clean of our past traumas with other teachers first. Entering the studio with fears and engrained limiting beliefs because of what so-and-so said 5 years ago is just as bad as starting a new relationship while still harboring issues from our exes. Excavate the bones from when you were a student and examine them closely for the lessons that they can give you.

First and foremost understand that there is a 90% chance that the incident had nothing to with you. Your past teacher or mentor may have been acting out of perceived fear. For example, you weren't put into the show because your teacher was afraid you'd mess up and make them look bad. You were held back on purpose because your teacher was afraid of losing money. You were told you were doing it wrong because your teacher was afraid of not looking intelligent. What is the common denominator here? Ego.

Ego is typically defined as one's sense of self-importance or identity. Unfortunately this plays a large role in teaching and in my opinion defines how effective a tecaher can be.

We must come to terms with the effect our past mentor's egoes may still have on us in order to not repeat the same mistakes or even pass down the same negative information to our own students. Usually this ego stain shows up in the form of our own inner negative self talk that pops up when we are trying to advance ourselves.

"I think I should teach a sword workshop."

What are you talking about? You dropped the sword at the last show!

"I love that costume!"

That wouldn't look good on you. It's not flattering for your body type.

"I'm nervous, but I think I should audition for that."

You should take more lessons instead. You're not ready.

"I wonder if that restaurant is hiring dancers."

Your zilling sounds a little crazy, don't you think?

Your teachers may have never said these awful things verbatim, but your inner self-critic is sneaky. It's not really about the words that were said, inner voice picks up on the way someone made you *feel*. Intonation, body language, inflection, *the vibe*. That's really what sticks with us. It's crucial to understand that how someone made us feel have even been unintentional or in passing. Even teachers are subject to having their heads in the cloud or not being self-aware of the implication of how they are coming across. It's also possible that they are just a downright awful person.

The first step is to identify where these little mind monsters are coming from. It may be several people or just one person, but let's do the work to identify them. They are the villian(s) in your story. Now, DE-villainize them! The longer someone holds that role in your mind, the more power they have over you. Yes, this is easier said than done. It will take time to clear the cobwebs so be patient with yourself and mindful of when the voice pops up. When it does, make an action plan. Come up with three things that you can do to silence the voice and prove to yourself that you can do it.

"I want to start teaching."

You? Are you ready for that? You're not a famous performer. You don't own a studio.

"I do not own a studio. But, I can research opening one. I will also go to other studios in the area and see if they are hiring. I will then work on my promotion skills to get my name out more."

But your students will question you. You need more lessons.

"I will continue lessons or find more on what I want to teach. If I don't know the answer to something in class, we will research it together or I will ask a trusted source that I know."

Continue this conversation until your inner critic runs out of options. Write down your ideas and plans and follow up on them. Eventually, your conversations will get shorter and your productivity will skyrocket.

Having a good support network is also key when you begin teaching. You may run into situations with students that you didn't expect and fall outside the academic realms. Typically, our students lead normal lives outside of their dance classes and will often drop their emotional baggage into the studio. Adult dance classes in particular are usually right after work hours and students shuffle in still wearing their work clothes, laden down with the emotions of the day. I've had students burst into tears in the middle of class because a boss yelled at them right before they came in.

You may also hear about significant others, children, family drama, divorces, illness and financial distress. We're human. As teachers it's important to take into account that people take dance classes for social reasons, too. It's not unreasonable for people to form friendships within a class and begin to discuss aspects of their lives. It's also natural for adult students to still look up to you as an authority figure and source of comfort. You will have students that barely talk, and you will also have students that are clearly looking for a source of inspiration. You may also have students that behave strangely out of nervousness, such as talking over you or making weird comments. You could even have the rare student that challenges you! You'll think to yourself, why did this person sign up for class?

This is where knowing other teachers, professional dancers or even being part of online forums can help should you encounter a student issue that you can't handle or need further advice on. Usually, common sense goes a long way and it's ok to be friends with students but you can still have a comfortable distance and remain professional within the classroom.

I've been fortunate to not encounter a lot of student drama in my career but we all have pitfalls. Whether it's a misunderstanding or a complete disagreement within core values, the best you can do is offer an apology and compassion unless things become unreasonable.

The reality is that everyone wants to feel accepted and understood. Be prepared to stay a little bit after class, and wipe a few tears occasionally. As I've said a million times at this point , you don't need to have any answers. Just be an open ear and a safe space. Call on your own resources if necessary. The healthy tree provides shade for others.

CHAPTER 6

Body Talk

———◦———

This next chapter is for students, performers and teachers. Well, ok. It's for everyone.

Bellydance has a serious image problem.

We are told during our formative beginning stages that "bellydance is for everyone!" We buy class packages and encourage ourselves to try a sensual artform because "bellydance is made for a woman's body!" and "classes are suitable for all body types." We see and attend almost ritualistic women's dance circles celebrating the divine feminine within us all that is reconnecting to this ancient beautiful sacred artform.

And yet...

All of the promotional images show tanned, young and svelte ladies that have clearly not had children. The restuarants and entertainment productions hire the beautiful and young sometimes with no clear indication that they even looked at their talents. There are no people of color. Men are made fun of. Non-Binary, Trans and Gender Queer are given confused looks.

I thought....Bellydance was for everyone?

Somewhere between buying our first costume and doing our first professional gigs the good vibes start to run out. You've been taking Bellydance classes for years and then all of a sudden someone will say to you, "You don't look like a Bellydancer!" It doesn't take long before you start to feel like your Inner Goddess can only come out if you have a flat tummy and long dark hair.

Do not get me wrong. Women's circles and Goddess archetypes are a needed service in our modern age. There is no denying that women need a source of comfort, safety and mode of expression that they can sumptuously blossom in as their authentic selves. The issue is when only one specific image of a woman as Goddess or otherwise Ideal is pictured. It then becomes a single story narrative that has lasting consequences and unfortunately misses the original point. Instead of empowering, it becomes discriminatory. Instead of encouraging strength, it encourages bias. It also completely ignores bellydance for what it actually is; a folkloric based dance practiced by many people who form a living culture.

We hear proof of it all the time. "I've never seen a black/plus size/asian/male/trans/tall/short/ pale etc etc bellydancer before! Is this a fun hobby for you?" How deflating. Not only has it become such a radical idea for a bellydancer to look like anything else than a singular idea but it is also not thought of as possible to be a professional at it if you are outside of that idea.

I have had so many students come to me concerned before they even begin that they will be outcast or marginalized for who they are. The "community" that we once sought solace in now becomes the briar patch at the bottom of the jump. Will I be accepted? Should I market myself as a "different" bellydancer? What do I do if I can't find my place?

Let me give you a great, big hug with my thoughts! You are not "different." We are all "different." Ergo, none of us are "different." This imaginary dancing lady that we are all being held to in comparison does not exist. When someone says to you "You weren't what I was expecting." say back to them, "Were you expecting Princess Jasmine?" with a coy smile and watch them chuckle or look away in embarassment. Yes there are some famous dancers out there that seem to fit that mold and that's great for them. It's not a detriment to their character if they happen (or work hard) to fit into a societal belief of how things should be. It's also not a detriment to your character if you don't or don't care to.

There is a tendency to think that because we are in "Bellydanceland" as I like to call it, the rules of society and the Universe are suspended and we exist somehow on our own glittery island devoid of social norms. This is simply not so. What do we do if we are looking for new friends? Or a romantic partner? Or even a new job? We begin by establishing our values and what makes us unique. Imagine that, we think about our uniqueness! And then, we go out in search of whatever it is that matches or compliments our uniqueness.

This is how to rest of the world works! We don't focus on being different and then go sign up on a dating site complaining in our bio how terrible and weird and strange we are. We go on the site made for people like ourselves , fill out all the forms based on what WE want, and then look through OTHER people's lives trying to match them up with US.

Are you starting to get it now? A simple shift in mindset can make all of the difference but it's important to realize this idea of having to be a "certain way" is self imposed in our own culture. I know I'm one to talk. Anyone who knows me knows that I've had my bouts of self-doubt and body issues. I've heard the rude remarks and been turned down by clients and other dancers for roles in shows and gigs. When you Google "plus-size bellydancer," my image is in the Top 20. And yeah, it really stung. I[ve certainly cried a lot of tears feeling I just didn't fit in and I was barking up the wrong tree. I used to joke, "I hate my stomach, and I became a BELLYdancer. I am a GENIUS!"

I began to shift my mindset once I realized that I was not the only one who felt this way. I began to write articles, create inspirational posts and incorporate confidence building into my classes. I even made "body positive" part of my tagline. You know who responded? The massive amount of women who also felt that they had been slighted and were struggling to feel accepted. And not all of them were plus sized either. Sure, I was made fun of after that, but now I had the confidence weapon at my side. And on it's handle read, "You are NEVER alone."

I once had a student sheepishly come up to me confessing that she wanted to start teaching. But she felt shy and afraid. "I'm black and plus-sized, who on Earth will want to take classes with me?"

"Black, plus-sized women." I said flatly. She blinked a few times.

"But...I don't know any black, plus-sized female bellydancers." She said.

"Because you haven't taught them yet!"

75

She started her classes a few weeks later. Her first class photo was all black, plus-sized women who absolutely adored her.

Like does attract like such as in this case. But you will find, I promise, that even people that don't seem to be like you will find something in you that they resonate with.

Sometimes, it is merely your boldness. What you think is your biggest weid quality can be someone else's inspiration.

I often hear "bloom where you are planted" and "Go where you are celebrated." Quite true but this is not the whole picture. They still imply that there are certain mountains you cannot climb and places you cannot go. It would be more accurate to say "Plant your own garden" and "Create your own celebration."

Let's take the restaurant dancing gigs for example. They are without a doubt the most typical type of gig to aspire towards, especially for budding performers. They are also usually the fussiest about who they hire. Now, what makes you unique? Are you trans? Contact your local advocacy agency and then go in and pitch your idea for a magnificent night for LGBTQA that will bring a whole new demographic and clientele into their business. You know what? They might say no. Keep trying. Go to the next one. Go back to that advocacy and ask for advice. Tell your friends. The restuarant you initially approached may say no, but I guarantee there's a small business run by a lovely gay couple that would be overjoyed to have you. That's what "Go where you are celebrated" really means.

Guess what? There's more good news! Once that is done, now more people know about it. Then more people, and more people, and even more! And the more that know, the more that hive mind gets tapped, the more people just like you come out of the woodwork to support you.

We are afraid of judgement. We are afraid of not belonging. The need to feel a part of something larger than ourselves is fundamental to human consciousness. Our early memories of the fear of not belonging most likely started in school, our first exposure to the outside world beyond our nuclear families. We may continue to hear the same terrible bullying from politicians and news casts. It may feel like a tremendous burden to carry the torch of being "that dancer." The question is, will you carry the torch or do nothing and always wonder what you could have done?

Carrying the torch may be arduous at times but it doesn't need to be a terrifying venture at all times. The internet is many things, but it is also a tool. Use it to find people, places and things that create the experience you want to have. Usually our fears of not fitting in are stemming from being bombareded by thousands of images of what we're not. You are not required by any entity to view, follow, like, engage with anything that is not bringing you joy. Not famous bellydancers. Not local groups. Not this or that popular thing.

Find, follow, like and engage with people, places, and things that make you feel cozy, inspired and welcomed. You can always add the other stuff back in later. For now, and in your low points, you need to feel included in the dialogue. Do a media cleanse. The images and words we see all day become part of our inner dialogue that transmutes into our feelings of where we see ourselves in the outer landscape. If you never hae the opportunity to see a glimpse of yourself in the bellydance scene, your mind is fighting a losing battle.

Maybe your "uniqueness" is something that you haven't comes to terms with like a medical condition or a belief system. Maybe you haven't come out. Or maybe you just don't like talking about it. There are probably others interested in bellydance with that same "Thing," but there are also lots of other people not in Bellydanceland with the Thing that wouldn't mind helping you being a bellydancer with it.

Flip the script. You don't want to champion your Thing. You don't want to be the bellydancer with the Thing, the This or That bellydancer, with That Thing always being connected to your name and image. In the case of a medical condition, you may not be ready to go public and become the poster child of it. You are more than That Whatever Thing.

There is no requirement to use a label on yourself. However, there are two things that could happen. The Thing gets attached to you anyway because it's noticable or you could end dealing with the thing in silence and thereby make your anxiety about it worse. In either case you will need to be prepared for it. The best middle ground is to have a small group of trusted friends or mentors that you can embrace The Thing with. Not everything needs to be on the Global scale.

Above all, remember that you can be a force for change no matter how hard you want to fight your own fight. Encourage diversity and inclusion around you, support others with similar goals and other dancers that remind you of yourself. Recommend and ask for diverse dancers in troupes, productions and in features. If you see discrimination, speak up or do not support the offending party. By helping others, you make more room for everyone including yourself.

Finally, in the words of glamorously glittery singer Dolly Parton, "Dumb Blonde jokes don't offend me because I know I'm not dumb. I also know that I'm not blonde."

P.S. You'll notice I didn't include any notes on "this is the way the entertainment industry has always been so it's going to be hard..." At one time, drinking fountains were seperated by skin color. Just because that's how it's been does not mean it cannot be made better to include others. We can, and will, do better.

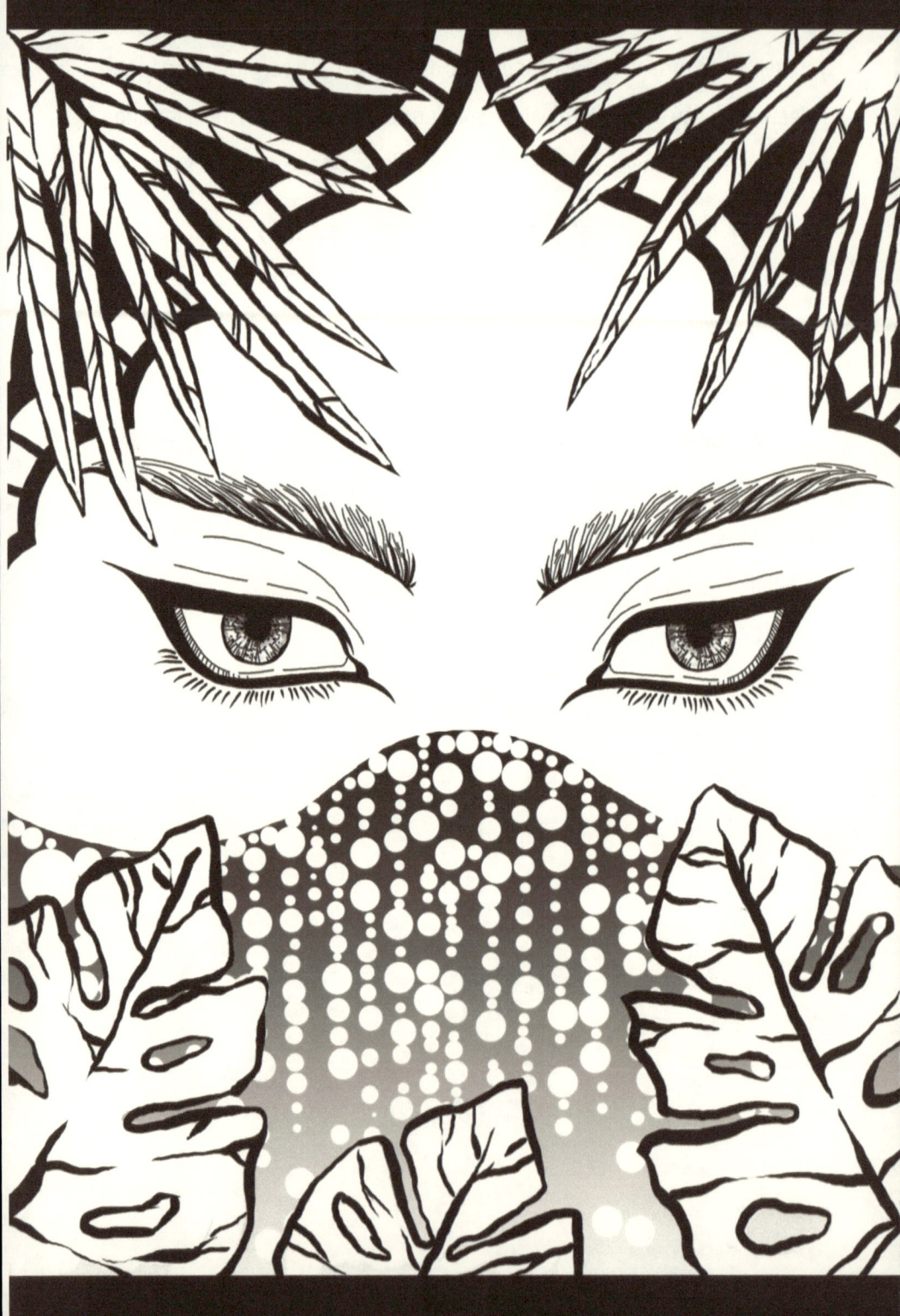

CHAPTER 7

Staying Motivated

One of friends and long time co-dancers, Lucie, and I have this occasional ritual where we get together at her place to snuggle her puppy and have what we call "Tea and Zills." Unlike myself, she is not much of a coffee drinker so we have tea instead and queue up bellydance instructional videos to practice. I actually learned how to zill doing this with her.

Typically we spend about 30 minutes actually dancing and then several hours catching up on the latest Bellydanceland drama and news. Lucie has always been good for mys oul because she views me in the light that I should have really seen myself all along. "You're a go getter! You just go out and do it! " She'll usually say to me while her dog plays with her hair ties. I will usually go to say that while I absolutely believe in just taking the leap and following dreams, it does come with it's pitfalls along the way that I do get stumped on.

One day, while talking about bellydance podcasts and how the topic of burn out gets brought up an awful lot, she looked at me and said, "You deal with a lot of garbage. How do you stay motivated?"

I instantly zoomed back in my mind to how many times I wondered if I could just quit and walk away, cried myself to sleep, how many nasty emails I'd gotten, rude comments, an honest-to-goodness stalker, the times I ate and drank my feelings and how many pillows I had beaten up in the course of my being a director and show producer. What the hell did keep me motivated all this time?

I responded somewhat solemnly, "Well, I really love this dance. I love the music, the movements, the feeling that I get when I perform. I'm my real me when I'm on stage."

Boom. Truth Bomb.

I continued, " When I get down, and I feel like hanging it up, I'm really grateful that I let some people go and found people like myself. I formed this team around me that thinks alike and supports each other when things get rough and doesn't judge each other for reacting. I can go to any of them and cry my eyes out and it's instantly game plan time and we're forming an action plan to make it better. That's how I keep going."

EPIC BOOM. Mushroom Cloud-inducing Truth Bomb to end all Truth Bombs.

Ever notice there's a lot of chatter in the "community" about toxicity and avoiding burn out? Ever notice there's also an equal amount of chatter about remaining perpetually positive and "good vibes only" even though anyone that seems to go against that grain get anything but good vibes in a tyrade that looks and feels a lot like The Crucible?

When we talk about motivation in Bellydance what we're really circling around is how to navigate through the muck of nonsense that is low vibrational stinky old jealousy and cattiness and come out smelling like a rose.

I'm sorry to say there's no exact science to it. First, we have to consider that Bellydance seems to be pretty unique even in entertainment industry terms. We scold each other for not attending events we don't care about and not liking people we don't like. We shame each other for being mad, pointing out issues and telling the truth. I'm not a fan of "call-out culture" and that's not what I'm referring to. I'm talking about coming down on people when they ask why it's suddenly become a thing to pay to perform in a hafla or for turning down working with someone because they personally have had a bad experience with them. Why do we continually lash out at our "sisters" to the point that we are all afraid to talk?

You'll notice the verbage I'm using here. Terms like "community" and "sisterhood" are used to slice and dice each other instead of what they really should mean. The "you can't sit with us" mentality is not a product of normal ad naturally-occuring group-building or friendships. Toxicity is created when each person in a community wants to exact revenge for feeling slighted in some way. Like kids in the sandbox we think Susie came in and encroached too far next to our sand castle and we need to show her what's up. We will build a bigger, better sand castle and little Susie will be left out in the cold with her little puny sand shack.

Listen, we are all guilty of this at some point or another. Myself included, sad to say. The environment that we have created may have started with good intentions but it has become a game of bellydance musical chairs. There is a growing feeling that the chairs are disappearing and we are all looking for validation that we are doing something right. No one wants to feel like they've spent all this time and money for nothing and that they will be acknowledged. Teachers become possessive of their students to the point of holding them down and over charging them. Dancers become catty and nasty with each other. Unhealthy obsessiveness with checking up on what everyone else is doing takes over people's time. And it all gets published on Facebook.

You cannot control what other people do.

I repeat. You have no control whatsoever over what other people do. Their actions. Their objectives. Their thoughts. Their decisions.

This can be a hard pill to swallow. We would all love if our students took the artform seriously, if undercutters disappeared and if venue owners would just get their ever-loving shcizz together. But, here we are. Just ourselves. The only person that you can control is you.

Yes, it is true that an awful lot of problems are small ones that we create ourselves. Before you lash out like a harpy make sure that you did not, in fact, just read the text wrong or that you aren't just projecting your own feelings into the mix. Stand back, take a deep breath and ask yourself if it's worth it or if you just need to say, "I'm sorry, do I understand you correctly?"

This is not to say that you must wipe away negative thoughts as flyaways that you are just being absurd for having. Your gut will tell you. You will cry. You will get angry. You will beat a pillow into submission. You will very likely call up your best friend and drink cheap wine together and complain about what happened. As you absolutely should. With the people who are on your A-team, in your corner, ready to come up with solutions and commiserate with your feelings. Your feelings are valid, you are having them for a reason. This is the best time for your assembled team of superheroes to swoop in and remind you of all of your goals and aspirations and get you back on track!

See, if you go off and whine to just another whiner, all you've done is whine. And all of that whining leads to that great, big gaping void of entitlement that we see in others. Everyone wants to be acknowledged and accepted. But, this whining and moaning groaning mentality that everything is unfair has led to the crybaby atittudes of our biggest soul suckers in the community. When did everyone start demanding trophies for 12th place? When we started giving it to them. By being persuaded that we were all just big meanie-heads with no sense of "sisterhood" the scene was systematically degraded into everyone having to assume equal footing. Which means, you guessed it, the minute someone tries to blast off and shake up the status quo... it's burn at the stake o'clock.

This is called by therapists and self-help gurus alike, "The Crab Effect." Basically, it refers to a phenomenon that when a bunch of crabs are dumped into a bucket they all start scuttling around until a brave one decides to try to climb out. The other crabs in the bucket will then turn their entire focus to *dragging that crab back down* to stay with the group in what is the most counter intuitive group manuever ever. The brave crab's efforts undermined, the certain doom of the entire collective group is ensured. No one gets out.

This analogy is used when members of a particular group attempt to reduce the self-confidence of any member who achieves success beyond the others. Whether it's out of envy, resentment, spite, conspiracy, or competitiveness in order to halt the individual's progress. It is the ultimate example of, "If I can't have it, no one can!" Take a quick gander into any Facebook discussion group and you'll see the number comment about why people leave Bellydance, or are thinking of leaving, has nothing to do with the dance itself.

"I love bellydance, but I can't handle Bellydancers anymore!"

Sadly, so many don't even realize they are enacting this bahavior onto their students or dance teams. It is up to each of us as dancers to remember that comparison is the thief of joy. No one has stolen anything from you, and you are not stealing from others by being successful. You earn exactly what you work for, and what fits you best. If you feel someone's pinchers on you, kick them off and get out of the bucket. If you have your pinchers in someone else, let go. As auther Mark Twain said, "Keep away from those who try to belittle your ambitions. Small people always do that, but the really great make you believe that you too can become great."

Conversely, our students are hooked into someone elses' Great IdeaTM or Dance SystemTM as a way to attain recognition and feel special. By paying someone else to tell us what level we are and where we fit in, we can stay in our nice, cozy cocoons of comfortable submission. Never seeing our own name in lights, we snugly feel secure in someone else's shadow as we wave our papers in other's faces. Some certifications serve real purposes: you need them to actually, physically do the job you wish to do. As in, you won't get hired without them. But ask yourself, did Samia Gamal have a Level 2 certification that she paid dues on from the School of WhozyWhatsIt, Nebraska?

You have got to have your A-Team ready. Joseph Campbell's myth cycle is a great one to study when it comes to understanding that no one can go it alone. The Hero's Journey inspired many great stories, famously including Star Wars. Think about it, what story had you read, what video game have you played, in which the hero did not have a satchel full of potions, a talking horse, an enchanted magical weapon and least three team mates. Of which included a healer, a mage, and probably a brute who could take whatever was leveled at him.

That corny saying "Life is about dancing in the rain" is true. The storms are coming. You know they're coming. Don't complain when you get wet and didn't have your umbrella ready after you first saw the clouds forming. And then feel the need to buy someone else's UmbrellaTM.

You have got to have your A-Team ready! Ready to dry your tears, wipe your snotty nose and pick you up when you're feeling like charred croquettes after Medusa the studio owner sent you a nasty email. This isn't about having an entourage of yes-men around you. It's about having a Plan, and setting yourself up for sucess.

I'm going to share an embarrassing story with you, but it will illustrate the point in several ways.

When I was 14, my Mother had met my step-father at that point and he was very gung-ho about travel. My Mother, being prudent in the financial department, finally relented and we took our first ever family vacation. We went on a cruise to the carribbean! We were completely clueless tourists in every way imaginable.

One of the shore excursions in the Cayman Islands was to ride The Banana Boat. You read that right. I do not remember the conversation, or what tropical drinks lead to this decision, but my mom and I decided that strapping ourselves to a giant, inflatable banana being pulled by a speedboat at a high rate of speed across the ocean was an excellent idea. What could possibly go wrong?

Fast forward to the actual event. We were indeed on a giant, yellow, inflatable banana boat with about ten other idiots robbed of their money but we were not strapped in. Grasping onto two tiny nylon straps that were kind of attached to the giant, inflatable banana between our legs we looked at each other with great anxiety. I had foolishly asked earlier as we were instructed to wear lifevests why we had to wear them during the whole ride.

The speedboat dragged us out to deeper waters, it's banana tourist passengers already wobbling to stay on at low velocity. Then, the boat opened up and we took off; a giant inflatable banana dashing across the surface of the beautiful blue ocean. Hitting every single wave along the way like hard speedbumps.

I was the youngest and had been positioned at the front of the banana, my little fourteen year old arms straining to hang on to the tiny nylon straps as wave after wave was thrust against us until they completely gave out. I went flying into the ocean like a baseball. All I remember is a swirl of blue and white.

There was no time to close my eyes, prep my body or even take a final gasp of air. Down I went.

When I finally bobbed up to the surface, thanks to my lifevest, I realized that everyone else had fallen off too. Peppered across the surface of the sea, the Banana Boat had totally peeled apart. Split, if you will. My mother was in complete hysterics seaching for me. They were so far away from where I had originally been thrown into the sea that she thought I had drowned. I saw her tiny head and body in the distance combing the water around her frantically. I had been under the water for a lot longer than it seemed.

It was embarrassing for me to wait until the speedboat came by to collect us all. I felt like it was all my fault. If I just could have hung on tighter. If I was just stronger. I had caused a chain reaction by not being able to hang on. My body weight suddenly missing at the front of this obviously well-engineered giant banana had caused the whole thing to capsize and throw everyone off. I had ruined the fun for everyone.

There are several morals to this story. First of all, giant bananas do not make good boats.

Secondly, this future bellydancer was saved by a lifevest. Because of that lifevest that I complained about earlier was on my person, I was able to bob up to the surface naturally and worry free. Even though I had been completely taken off gaurd and thrust into an unknown situation within a split second, *there was a support system in place to protect me.* Your A-team is your lifevest.

Who is your A-team? If your best five friends were high school yearbook superlatives, who would they be?

The best person to go to in an emergency:

The best person to cry with:

The best person to get angry with:

The most organized, ready to go one:

The one the reminds you most of yourself:

Thirdly, I felt guilty. This is important. Sometimes things happen and it will be our perception that it was our fault. Or we will be made to feel like it was our fault. The reality is, and was, it's no one's fault but the guy who owned and sold tickets for a giant, inflatable banana and put a minor at the front of the peel. Your A-team will be there to shake sense back into you and make sure you're seeing things clearly rather than letting you mope around thinking everything icky in your dance career is solely on you. A good A-team will help you determine what is yours to control and will then help form a plan to correct it. No judgement, maybe a few bad jokes and appetizers.

One of the heroes in my A-team, Zoe, started in the entertainment industry before she could even vote. She was signed to Sony entertainment when she was 16 as wannabe teen idol pop singer. Her early demo tapes are hysterical to listen to now, since we now know her as a Rave DJ, touring hardcore artist and fusion bellydancer. I like to think someday we'll be the two old showgirls wearing fur coats and fuzzy mules drinking cocktails by the pool reminiscing on all the old dirt back in the day. Because will any of this really matter when we've retired?

Anyway, something she likes to tell me when things start looking grey is that she once picked another recording artist's brain about how to keep it all straight. Sometimes, we just can't see the forest through the trees in the confusion of all the comings and goings. Or, we feel like we're just lost in the forest and perpetually walking in circles. Did I pass that rock before?

He told her something she wouldn't get for a few years, when the music industry had beaten her up a little more. He said, "It's all a chess board. Zoom out, and look at where all the players are. Then you'll see why they made that move, and what they're probably going to do next. More importantly, you''ll know what move you should make." Of course at first she thought this guy had taken some special pills at the last gig, but after a while she told me it all made sense. If you stand back and remove yourself (and your emotions) from a situation, you will start to see that everyone brought their emotions to the table and that's why move the way that they do. And then, you may react and move accordingly. Sometimes, it can even take our own anger out of the situation. We'll see the offenders for who they really are; scared, insecure, angry, tired, broke, lonely and freaking out.

Let me remind you not to be too concerned with the small potatoes. Not every ill timed comment or eye roll perfromance deserves your utmost vexation and you'll need to learn how to fight your battles. Sure, I get annoyed when people wearing Harem Girl Halloween Costumes show up on club podiums and wiggle around. Annoying, but not worth your time. Often the things that annoy us on such a base level get under our skin because of a larger reason than what we're actually seeing. After all, if that club wanted (or cared) about real Bellydancers, finding them was only a quick Google search away.

I'll also remind you that if you actually do take a misstep and talk out of turn, say something you don't mean or say something that was taken the wrong way just go ahead and apologize. Even if you think it was perfectly clear, Becky! Save yourself the headache if having it blow up into a screenshot nightmare by just saying, "Oh, I'm so sorry if came off that way! What I meant to say was...."

There are a couple of tools that I ironically picked up from being in an abusive relationship, or have stumbled upon in my travels, that I have reworked to fit into Bellydance Drama Scenarios. If you really want to know how I've made it this far, lean in.

1. Avoidance.

This is not a popular one. In Bellydanceland we're all FRIIIEEENNNDDSSSS. Not talking to each other is seen by a fair amount of people to be the ultimate in rudeness and not acceptable. I'm here to tell you if you are being harassed or someone generallly rubs you the wrong way so much that being around them makes your skin crawl you don't need to talk to them, follow them on Facebook, attend their events or be FRRRIIIEEENNNDDDSSS. If it requires fake smiling on your part, rethink it. Especially in the cases of the truly malicious, stay away at any and all costs. This seems to feel cold for a lot of people, so it's helpful to think of it as protecting yourself and not harming the other person. You can love someone from a distance. Tough love is still love and cordial, brief, conversations at social gatherings are just fine. Then excuse yourself to the loo.

Do not make false promises to "hang out later," or "catch up sometime over coffee!" Just a simple "Nice to hear from you" and that's it. This is especially true if the culprit is family, or just someone who always happens to be at the studio when you are. You can still love them, but you'll do it from over there and on your terms.

2. Drop the Rope

This is a fun one and gets to be filed under "How to play games with your Bully's mind." There's a popular saying that goes "The best way to win with a toxic person is to not play the game." And that's exactly right. Drop the Rope is a term refering to the game tug of war, and is a method employed by psychologists and therapists for diffusing everything from custody battles to workplace drama. Imagine two warring parties playing tug of war, each person has the rope in their hand. As long both people keeping pulling, the drama ensues, eventually spiraling into one person winning by pulling the other person to their side. Meaning, ensnaring the other person into their drama. The best way to ensure you don't get caught up is to *drop the rope.* By the dropping the rope, there is no tug of war. The game is over. No one has won. Well, actually you won because you took control of the situation by basically obliterating the situation from continuing to happen. How do you drop the rope? Excuse yourself from the room. Pretend you can't hear them, the music is too loud. Walk away. Leave the message on read. Leave the Facebook group. Click Unfollow. Or my personal favorite: Just say "Ok." This is especially beneficial when someone is trying to get you to react by provoking you. A word of caution however, they may continue to try to provoke you because they are having a hissy fit and haven't gotten the rise out of you that they wanted. Keep dropping the rope, begin avoidance and alert your A-team and the authorities if it gets out of hand.

3. The Grey Rock Method

This one is more serious. Not in it's execution; it's actually simple in it's design. The Grey Rock Method was orginally designed for use with narcicissts, sociopaths, and psychopaths. The slimiest of the slimey. If you aren't sure what that means, think of a situation where the offender is not only trying to get a rise out of you, they are hellbent on destroying your image, creating rumors, slander and all kinds of other incredibly hateful stuff. This one is for the active fruitcake that definitely wants to corner you. You're already using avoidance but somehow you ended up taking the same workshop together and you're dreading it. Or, you are trying to get out the restaurant gig and you need to have that final conversation. You get the idea. This method requires a little thinking ahead. In every scenario that this is employed you've already had bad experiences with the offender and know what they are like. There is no doubt as to their intention. You cannot feel sorry for yourself, or that you somehow deserve this treatment. They want you to think those things about yourself, so that you will slip up and feed them their favorite food. Your pain. Use total avoidance if you have not reached this point yet.

Think ahead: what will you say if you see them again? Then get ready for the acting performance of your life. Ready? You want to be as boring as possible. Like a Gray Rock! There is nothing special about you. You are nothing more than a fleshbag wondering the planet looking to meet your basic needs. You haven't done anything at all lately. You never leave the house. You have no friends. You have no life. You are no one. And then keep talking about how boring you are! Drone on and on about it like the world depends on it. You will literally snooze them to death.

Yikes that sounds counter intuitive right? Listen carefully. The real nasties out there, the sociopaths and what Princess Farhana calls the Professional Underminers, feed on shiny things. Their sole drive is to make themselves feel better by taking down the shiny people so that they may bask in the glory that they defeated the Great SoandSo. By remaining as boing as possible, you are doing the human equivalent of "playing dead." You are no longer as shiny, and they have a much harder time controlling your feelings.

Here's the real kicker. Sometimes a person like this can come off as all sweet and caring and will garnish their messages with 200 emojis and a chipper "Hey Girl!" Remember what I said earlier? Follow your gut.

Example.

Offender: "Hey Jane, I know how much you wanted to be in the show, and that we decided that you weren't the right fit because of your lower skill level. (I know so many movers and shakers!) But we did have an opening come up. Since this is such an awesome opportunity and I know you need help with your dance skills, I think we can fit you in! You'll need to purchase two workshops, and since you are still a student we'll sell you a DVD from the shop at half price. Send me your music and I'll see you there! :) :) :) "

You, using Grey Rock: "Thanks for getting back to me. I wish I could. Unfortunately something came up. I have to get a root canal done at 7 am that day, and then little Jimmy has soccer practice until late. DVD's have gotten so expensive don't you think? I remember when they were cheap. Anyway, I'm pretty sure the car needs a tune up and I couldn't make it to the workshops. I've been dealing with terrible migraines lately and then realized the car was making this odd clicking sound.....

And on and on and on you go....whether it's via text or voice. No matter how they try to shift it back to something that irks you, keep going on about your boring, complicated, ho-hum life. If it gets really tough or you're out of material, find an excuse to end the conversation. Then go collect your Academy Award.

I have used this on toxic people of all stripes, but I will admit that the more you're in the public eye the harder it becomes. More than likely you've been scoped out on social media first and will be baraged with questions about this or that thing you're doing. Shrug it off and minimize it using the same method. "Oh that? That's nothing. It was no big deal. I left early." Under no circumstances are you to ask, "How about you?" The buck stops here.

4. The Dahlia Method

This is a doozy and is named after my friend Dahlia, who proposed this when I was struggling with a really conniving dancer I needed to let go from my team. She is the Director of a Burlesque troupe in my town (a scene that also has a hot bed of drama). When someone is being particulary heated and argumentative, to the point of having cyclical logic or being unreasonable, she will stop the conversation dead in it's tracks but repeatedly asking questions. "So what would you do in my situation?" "How would you have handled it?" "How would you feel if this happened to you?" She keeps asking these questions, silently listening to whatever cockamamie reponse they have until they literally run of answers. She can then determine the best course of action to further the conversation.

When I implemented this method, it led to silence so fast I was stunned. Of course the person kept trying to come back later to regain control of the conversation. I would simply repeat the question. Over. And over. And over. It's a little like training dogs or small children. We aren't moving forward until you've done the thing I'm asking. Or, conversely, when they do get silent, that's a great time to hit the Block button.

Finally, when it comes to motivation, the most important and utterly significant thing you can do is this: not lose sight of what you love about this dance.

The first said I said to Lucie when she asked me is that I love this dance. I love the music used for this dance. I love the movements of this dance. I love costumes of this dance. I love choreographing this dance. I love teaching this dance. I love the heart and soul of Egyptian dance. I live, breathe and eat it. And I do it on purpose. As much as possible. I pursue it with the unwaivering tenacity of a cheetah chasing a ghazelle. Every waking moment of every day I think, "Can I bellydance today?"

Even in my worst career days when I get a nasty phone call from a studio or I lose a teaching position; I love this dance. So and So is mean with me, or I don't get accepted into something I really, really wanted; I love this dance.

Above any and all things you have to find what you love in this artform. The quiz you took earlier on to determine your personality type is your lifeline. That is the set of core values that you hold dear and you cannot let them go. Not for anyone or anything or under any amount of pressure. If you go forward holding this holy grail of love for whatever it is in this artform, you will find a way. No matter what beasties or setbacks come at you if you keep that passion the path will present itself. A way will be made. You will never lack motivation, because you won't need to be motivated!

It took years of whittling out the toxic people, odd people, stray people, and just generally useless people from my life before I got to a place of cozy. Actually it's not cozy. It's a raging inferno of awesome that is constantly being fed with new ideas, business proposals, dreams, inspiration and gumption. Why? Because presently all of my social circles are filled with entrepreneurs, writers, motivational speakers, spiritual gurus, fitness gurus, dancers of all kinds, marketing experts, new moms, dreamers, and doers. This adds up the past couple of years of us all getting so much done for ourselves because we have generated a hive mind of bartering, encouraging, helping, listening and examining. My friends either share this love of the dance with me, or respect me for it and share their love of their thing with it. It is awesome. Who needs motivation when you live inside a well oiled entrepreneurial bellydance machine?

CHAPTER 8

Get Back to the Plan, Stan

Ok, this is it. Your costumes are ready and sparkling. Your business cards have arrived in the mail. Your website looks lovely. Your Facebook page is gaining more likes (thanks, mom!) and you are on fire choreographing and training your little jingly heart out.

And....here we wait. Grab a sandwich, this could take a while.

Comedian Eddie Cantor said, "It takes 20 years to make an overnight success." He's not kidding. Yes, we live in an age of Insta-Famous and oddball cat videos that suddenly become viral to the point that the owners need to get a lawyer. The lightning strike of Fame could strike you all at once; but more than likely it's going to be part of a brewing storm that lingers and has several little strikes along the way followed by rolling thunder that takes a while to be heard in the distance.

In the beginning as well as at different points in your career it will feel like what my mom calls a "thundering heard of turtles." You will feel stalled, like nothing is moving, and you will hear crickets in your inbox. So how do you know you're doing it right?

Chatter. The storm starts brewing when people start talking. They start commenting on your posts, likes go up, shares start happening, etc. That post you posted three weeks ago and forgot about gets brought up at the next social outing. People start asking you about what you're doing. "Have you met Oriana? She's a Bellydancer. Isn't that neat?" This is the best sign you can have. It's not enough to get your name lin front of people. People see names and faces all day long without a further thought. You have to get them curious and wanting to know more. If they are talking about it, and asking about it, that means they are inquisitive.

When you really get going an odd phenomenon happens. Your phone will start blowing up. With random messages. When is class? How much? Are you still doing this? Can I check back later? When is the next show? Omg I love your shirt! Hey do you want to get lunch? OMG we should go to this! It will feel overwhelming. And strange. Where is the money? Where are the bookings? Are you guys just lonely or are you going to actually see me bellydance?

This is where most normal people jump off the bus and head back to the haflas. It's a lot to deal with and frankly gets annoying real quick. Esepcially if you're already busy working a full time job with kids and an S.O. and gigging is supposed to be your side hustle. It will give you new insight as to why celebrities and CEO's hire assistants and spend their time being as inconspicuous as possible. Before you grab your oversized sunglassses and run for the hills; you need to know that this stage in unavoidable if you want to go further and that is why I always mention it to people when I'm talking about business. Remember, having people blow YOU UP is far better than making cold calls trying to get people to get interested in you. This is what the seed about to break through the soil looks like. Do not give up now!

Learning to delegate and prioritize has been my biggest lesson so I present it here with the compassion that I know how it feels to get burnt out putting everyone's messages before your own. I was so determined to fight the stigma that bellydancers were unapproachable and hard to communictae with that I pretty much had my cellphone surgically grafted to my hand at all times. Social media consumed my life and while I did become an expert at it, I wasn't making time for the things that really mattered like, ya know...dancing.

Here's some tips on managing the actual business of bellydance:

1. There's an app for that. Auto Responders, away messages and even business second phone line creators are wonderful for re routing the traffic and letting people know you got the message and will respond ASAP. It also makes you look way more professional than just not answering until you feel like it or leaving it on read.

2. If you are seriously getting a case of hives or it's triggering your anxiety to the max, hire someone. I'm not talking about just giving your nephew $5 and a pizza either. Unless your nephew really knows what he's doing. Get a Virtual Assistant or an Intern. I know it sounds all fancy schamncy and expensive but you have two choices: do it the right way yourself or get someone who can do it the right way. The more complicated the business, like owning a studio, the more important this becomes. Unanswered and unprofessionally answered messages and phone calls are lost money. I hired a Virtual Assistant when I ran

my first major workshop weekend. I was worried the promotion just wasn't getting out between juggling my part-time job, my own classes, the company's stuff and now this large event. It was seriously the best thing I ever did. If you feel like your phone is rather dry and you're not at the stage where you're ready to hand your passwords to someone and say "Please just steal my identity, I don't even care at this point," take advantage of this time to get situated with social media techniques and prepared for when messages do come in.

3. Set yourself up for success. When you set up your website, Facebook and other social platforms make it all of the messages all go to one email. Make a separate business email if you want. Then, disable notifications or even just the notification sound. Set up a routine for yourself to only check your accounts at certain times, when you are ready. You'll be thankful when your day isn't being interrupted by the constant dinging of useless, non-business related messages.

I guarantee 99% of your messages will come in via texts or personal messages. I've sealed entire contracts with people over messenger spread out over course of two hours because we were both also doing other things and could not call. This is our world now. Most people work multiple jobs and most of our communication is over text. It cannot be avoided. Irritating at times, yes, but necessary. Make the technology work for you.

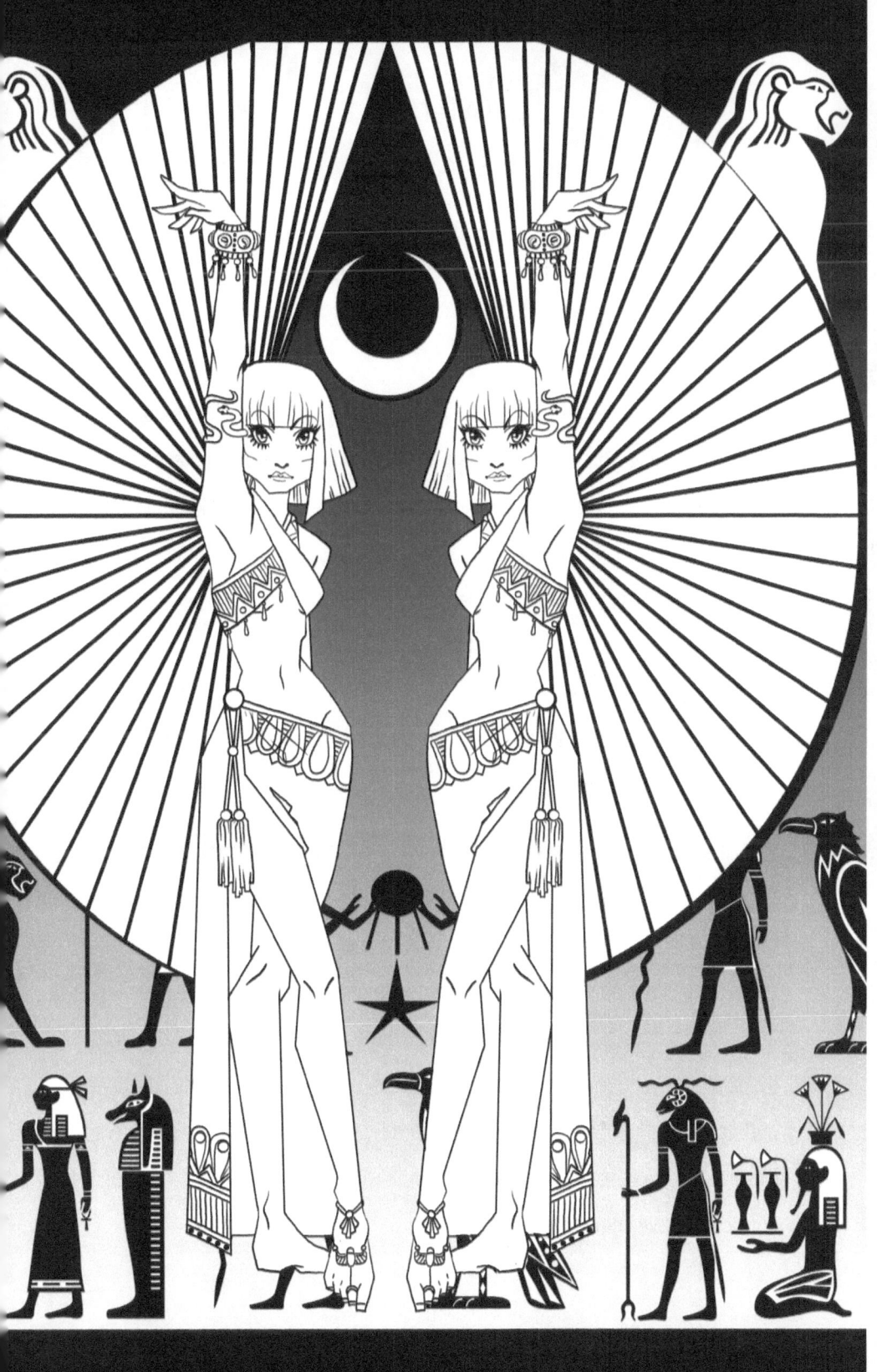

CHAPTER 9

The Choreography of YOU

In the hustle and bustle of figuring out different marketing techniques and pondering if you try Facebook ads it's very easy to become complacent in our dance training. We see this evidenced with the Old Showgirls that linger in every community. Burnt out, injured, raspy voiced and perpetually exhausted they limp from gig to gig wearing the same costumes, using the same songs and snapping at people along the way. Sure, they are performing every...single...weekend...but is this success? It's interesting that these are usually the same folks that are always complaining about money and never being happy either. Hmm.

This has admittedly been a hard one for me too. Having just gotten out of the phase of building my empire in Bellydanceland to going back to the drawing board in planning and development, I was on the verge of burn out. Marketing and analytics are an endless field of study. Uninspired, performing all the time and juggling several projects at once I had simultaneously met my goals from five years ago and missed the mark completely. I wasn't leaving my little town and getting OUT THERE. I wasn't creating new work and rubbing elbows with the greats. I wasn't sipping champagne with my gal pals watching Rio the pool boy scoop leaves out of the jacuzzi.

NOT YET ANYWAY.

Rest is crucial for artists. It's a concept that doesn't seem to be embraced in the American business world. It's go go go, work work work, and very often we are punished for using our vacation days that we earned. If we even get vacation days. Our vacation days have conditions. There are days we cannot use our vacation days. What's a vacation again?

The point is, and I know I sound like a total hypocrite, but you have to rest. You can hustle hustle hustle but what good is all of that hustling when you can't stop to smell the roses you hustled up? At the end of the day no matter how business savvy we become or how articulate, we are artists. The product we sell, proclaim, advertise and push is our art. And our art is an expression of ourselves.

By taking care of ourselves and continuing to fill our creative wells as we draw from them, we ensure that we can continue our inspired work for years to come.

The best way to do this is to continue to discover and unfold ourselves. Our real selves. The best bellydancer that we can be. Find the music that you really love and that draws something extra special out of you each and every time. Wear costumes that you feel scrumptious in. Learn to feel and divine the energy from your audience. We are lightning rods of energy and pendulums of deep feeling. The Bellydancer is the instrument of the Divine Source that at once feels their own senses while allowing those viewing to feel and experience theirs. This, I believe, is the real reason why we are often depicted with serpents. Symbols of transmutation we can shed our skins over and over again while still remaining ourselves. We glide and coil ourselves between creation and destruction, always guiding the ebb and flow of energy. It was never meant to be all give. Giving to the audience, giving to teachers, giving to students, giving to lovers, admirers, the crowd, the world. It's also not all taking either. Demanding attention, using shock tactics, making a scene or being a diva. It is supposed to be both give AND take. It is meant to be an exchange, an everlasting fertile conversation where dancer and viewer both can experience the most fundamental of all- human connection.

It's so easy to get swept up in wanting to be someone else or fit an expectation. "Today you are You, that is truer than true. There is no one alive who is Youer than You!" wrote Dr. Suess. He got it. As artists we are very hypercritical of ourselves. It is part of the creative process to always keep trying to improve and change and grow our sill level. Usually this ends up with us watching all of our own performance videos through our fingers and sometimes even walking off stage feeling a huge letdown that we know we didn't do what we think is good enough. These feelings deplete us. They drag us down until we kick rocks and feel like we'll just never get there. It takes a real brass pair to get up on a stage at any level, and do something that looks like art. As we advance the stakes only get higher and higher. It is perfectly ok to always want to aim higher and dig deeper; but you have to commit, right now, to radically accept the work you are doing as completely valid as long as you are giving it your all.

If you are trying to pour feeling and depth and musicality from an empty vessel you will end up not producing anything deep at all. You will be stiff, lackluster and flat out boring. You will be injured, tired, sick and going through the motions. Or even worse, you will become a miserable soul-sucking energy vampire with a black cloud over their head that pushes everyone away. You will be a total drag to watch and be around. You will be the exact opposite of everything you've been trying to do.

As I am writing this, I have a severe case of the flu. To illustrate my point that I am not just blowing smoke up your behind, I have worked myself to exhaustion. My immune system has cuddled up next to the Titanic at the bottom of the ocean floor and I was forced to gleefully hand over my classes to my co-dancers to sub or cancel them all together. I needed to refill myself, but my mind wasn't letting me so my body decided it had had enough of my crap and slammed on the brakes. Self-care is nothing to sneeze at (pardon the pun). It's not all mani-pedis and bath bombs either. Sometimes, it's the difference between losing your mind and staying in the game. No wonder celebrities collapse in exhaustion on stage.

Here are 10 relatively easy, but powerful, ways to refill your dance well:

1. Watch inspiring youtube videos of your favorite dancers
2. exchange new music with a friend, or get around to a song you always wanted to work on
3. design your dream costume: no budget! Tape the drawing up where you can see it
4. go online shopping with no intent to buy

5. get a big calendar and plan out all of the events you know you want to go to for the year

6. go look at other art. go to the museum, buy a new book, watch new movies, find a different type of music, go to a food festival, try a wine tasting, take a class in a different style of dance

7. Set up a DIY dance retreat! What kind of workshop have you always wished you could take? Spend time researching and watching that topic in depth. Grab a friend for more fun!

8. Get out of your normal routine. My early "studio" used to be the laundromat by my ghetto apartment in my 20's. I wrote some of my best choreography there.

9. Make a vision board

10. join an online challenge, or make your own! #drumsolo #omg

The amount of down time you need depends on you. As an artist I find myself to be at my most creative right the thrill of a big project finally being done and I ride that wave. Others find they experience a lull or a "letdown" after the rush of a big show is over. Listen to your body. Feed it, stretch it and rest it.

Now that you're all rested up and inspired and whatnot, you need a plan. You will not find the treasure without the map and the big red X is over your wildest dreams. Having a plan, a goal and a vision also helps you with you self-care routine. If something does fit into your vision and is not ultimately leading you towards your big red X, you are allowed to safely turn it down. Remember how I said earlier not everything is an opportunity? Sometimes people have trouble making decisions because making a decision means you had to cut out things that were not part of the decision. You have to choose. Accepting every and any thing is kind of like hoarding. You end up taking on everything that is presented to you with no idea if you'll use it later or what it's purpose is until one day you wake up next to the ceiling on top of a pile of random stuff and you can't find the cat. If it does not fit the vision, it cannot be on your list of things to do.

That doesn't mean your plan and your big red X have to be in serious, competitive Russian Olympic mode either. If doing the yearly charity hafla brings you great joy and fills you up with the warm fuzzies, it goes on the list.

I will share one big secret with you however, one that keeps me quite sane. It's a good idea to always have something to work on in your back pocket. Always have the proverbial Ace up your sleeve. You see the big names and Fortune 500 companies doing it all the time. Famous basketball players don't just play basketball. They have their own shoes, a breakfast cereal, they donate to charity, endorse products in commercials and cameo in sitcoms. It's simply called Diversification and while it sounds the opposite of my "don't overwhelm yourself" speech that I literally just gave you, hear me out.

Let's say your wildest dream that's buried under the big red X is to win a big competition. In Egypt. With all the big names watching you. Slightly terrifying, no? The dotted lines on your map may also have pitstops at learning Arabic, studying with world renowed teachers and costume design. That gives you opportunity to capatalize and diversify yourself. Teach Arabic to other bellydancers. Write a blog. Teach workshops on beading. Host your teachers so other people can study with them. None of these things have taken away from your vision and you'll have even more enriching experiences that will get you closer to your goal. Also, very important, if something doesn't pan out you have other things to fall back on. If you put all of your eggs in one basket waiting for that resturant gig to open up, what if it doesn't? What if you hate it and change your mind? What if they hate you and change their mind? Having diversity in your plan gives you options and the strength to know that if something is a dead end you still have something going on.

It can also be used for alternate sources of revenue, if needed. If your goal is to travel, you'll need to cover expenses. Monetizing something on the side that is still part of your overall vision helps you be self sustaining. Imagine being Paris Hilton. "Oh that song isn't doing so well on the charts? Hmph. Well, time to make another perfume." That's how the rich stay rich, companies stay afloat and you can keep yourself busy while adding to your impressive list of credentials. The key is making sure it brings you joy and it fits into the plan.

Let's play a fun game. Let's be celebrities! Or royalty, you pick. The name of this game is money is no option, there are no rules, and you are imagining your wildest dream. Be as detailed as you can possibly be. I've given you prompts as to what to write, but really get into it. Describe in great detail what you would do, have and see if there were no bounds.

I make limitless amounts of money effortlessly as a Bellydancer. I am world famous. The first thing I will do when I get up in the morning is_____(activity)_____with_____(thing)_____ _____. Then, I'll board my private jet to fly off to_____(place)_____. I am performing that night with my best friend _____(name)_____. My costume

is_____(color)_____and

dripping with _____(jewel)_____. It's a one of a kind

design by ____(name)_____ made exclusively for me. In

fact, we are designing _____(thing)_____ together to

launch next fall as part of my new product line. I've also been approached by a

perfume company to create my own scent! It will be called

____(name)_____ and will smell

like_____(scents)_____. After we're

done performing, the bestie and I will go to the best resturant in town, sit at

our private table and eat

_____(food)_____(strictly off-menu of course).

The next day I will begin working on my studio album, which is _____(type

of)_____ music and features my favorite singer,

_____(name)_____. Later this week, I need to buy a

new outfit at _____(brand or store)_____ for

a charity gala. I'm giving a presentation on ___(charitable

cause)_____ and want to look my best. I'm

thinking of wearing _____(article of clothing)_____ and

being ready for the red carpet! I'll be doing an interview with _____(magazine

or talk show)_____afterwards to spill all of the

details.

This is your wildest dream. Don't let me stop you, you can keep adding or subtracting onto this story for as long as you want, in as much detail as you want. You can vision board it, paint it, draw it, create the soundtrack for it. This is your big red X. Run towards it and live the life you've always imagined. Your life is your ultimate choreography and there is no more imporatnt factor in your dance than you. The real you. The best you that you can be. You are an incredible, beautiful, immensely talented bellydancer in an awful long line of incredible, beautiful and talented bellydancers.

CHAPTER 10

Finale

In conclusion, this dance is ancient. Bellydancers hold a very important place in the fabric of entertainment history and continue to incite mystery and awe. It's really no wonder that we are thought of in almost mythical terms. And watching us? Breathtaking. A real bellydancer giving her heart and soul to the music can make time stand still and bring all that watch her into a blurred state of spiritual ecstasy.

You deserve to show up, as your real self, and claim this spot in our lineage. A spot that was made for you, has been waiting for you and can only be filled by you. Your only masters are your mind, and the music that you dance to. Conquer both and you'll dance in greatness.

I leave you with a few quotes:

"Get your body out of the way and let your spirit soar!"- Ibrahim Farrah

"Oriental dance is an art of subtle expression. There are delicate shifting moods that coalesce to create feelings such as surprise, anger, shyness, fear, delight, disdain, pride and the sensuous. A good Oriental dancer must be able to depict darker shades within a man's heart as well- life and death, happiness and sorrow, all with great dignity. " - Nadia Gamal

"Dancers themselves are resposible for the good or bad reputation of the dance. Art itself is not good or bad, it's how the artist represents it. Art is art." - Mahmoud Reda

"One thing is for sure- this dance is not an isolated act in itself. It comes from a country and a culture." - Nourhan Sharif

Respect your teachers. Respect the culture. Respect your ancestors. Respect the homesick. Respect the people still dancing in the desert sands. Respect yourself.

Know your roots. Learn everything you can. And fearlessly dance the life you've always dreamed of.

Love,

Oriana

Epilogue by Shelley Parris Williams

There was this undeniable glow up that knitted our swaying bodies and dancing bare feet together that swept across the shiny wooden floors. The outpouring of school girl giggles and full belly laughs echoed throughout the room filling it from top to bottom. It was incredible to witness the magic unfolding on the peak of that mountaintop curtained by the panoramic view of the blue skies that seemed so close to our outstretched hands, that we could feel the clouds between our fingertips. Smiles being born on each woman's lips as she reconnected to the latent energy that swelled up from the earth's core as we awakened what once slept between our thighs and hips that those spiraling figure eights conjured up. Eyes closed being transported to worlds deep within as the music and Oriana's compassionate guidance made it safe enough to explore that sacred space confined within bodies vulnerable enough to go there. The tone had been set. It was okay to wrap arms around rolls, full hips and pudgy bellies in order to rise in love with the beauty of our perfectly imperfect curves and swerves. Oh, indeed it was absolute magic, to watch women discover their beauty and joy in the cadence of each powerful step!

When I close my eyes that is the image I am drawn to. That beautiful Saturday afternoon dancing with wildly, beautiful, Goddesses who had stepped into the invitation to be themselves in all of their fullness and glory. To Ignite their power and declare that they would Make SHIFT Happen from here on out. An experience I had VISIONed months prior, when some of my team and I had come to scout out the retreat site. Every class, workshop and meeting was designed for the women in attendance to have the most intimate encounter with themselves and the others they would share that sacred space with while we communed together in siSTARship. I knew without a doubt that Oriana had to facilitate a workshop for us during my retreat.

Oriana and I were kindred spirits. We had established a siSTAR, you my roomie in an alternate universe type of bond. We immediately hit it off following our first conversation by phone when my request for a bellydance teacher recommendation for our wellness center led me straight to her. I knew after that one phone call we would create some amazing things together. I had only taken one bellydance class a few years prior, but my dedicated work in supporting women to create a platform and container for radical selfCare and selfLove, to help heal trauma, and cultivate Emotional wellBEING and womb wellness had me seeking out more modalities to help facilitate and provide effective tools. I wanted them empowered and Oriana had carved out a beautiful practice in which women could explore those ideas with care, love and intention, all while laughing, having fun and at the same time loving their body. She packaged it all in such a way that the transformation that eventually takes place, has you striding by mirrors a little taller and more apt to stand in front of them a little longer admiring how far you've come on this journey of acceptance. Coming to place where you're no longer defined by the societal norms and rules as to who you should be and what you should look like according to their standards. I love this culture, tribe and movement Oriana has courageously armed with their own power and brought to the forefront. She is a champion for women to be FREE to authentically express themselves in spirit and in truth, to embrace the jiggle of our thighs and revel in their meeting together at the middle. To honor the stretch marks across our belly as the lines that hold our stories, some of which are still unspoken as we hadn't found the words just yet until she coaxed it out of us with each choreographed class. The classes which unwittingly began to reveal the choreography of our lives and how with each intentional step we were dancing out the isms of this life. Oriana invites you to be big, bold, light up the room and take up space unapologetically and all with a smile. She is grace personified and her passion and heart for this mission, this evolution that she sparks within each of us to step inside is so admirable. I love to watch her in action. I love to hear the voice she has given to so many who had went on for so long voiceless. She is a pioneer, a way bearer, inviting you to come along for the ride and be open to discover who you are. This book is just another declaration of how she is refashioning the ancient art of bellydance that may have lost its essence in its delivery to today's modern women. How it became diluted with unrealistic ideals and being held captive that it belonged only to a "select" few. Kudos to her for her bravery and brilliance for always seeing where those certain pieces are missing, and instead of waiting for someone else to come along and make it right, she has answered the call, with her divine yes and showed up with viable solutions. This book becomes a powerful tool in the hands of those who are ready to give their divine yes, show up and yield it!

About the Illustrator

Breanne Roberts is a multi-talented visual artist based in St. Petersburg, FL. She has exhibited numerous times locally and in print; she is known for her graphic, bold work with immense attention to detail. She is a graduate of the Pinellas County Center for the Arts and has studied Fine Art at the University of South Florida. She can be contacted at Neversummer2283@yahoo.com.

Rags to Riches

Dance with Passion, Achieve Success

Oriana Brooks

Forward by Tamalyn Dallal

Delve into the perfect starter manual to your bellydance career!
Whether you are just starting out, a seasoned professional, or thinki
of teaching; Raqs to Riches has tools and advice for every
Middle Eastern Dancer. One part self-help, one part motivation, ar
one part business advice, Oriana has devised this easy to follow an
inclusive guide for your next dance adventures.

Featuring a Foreword by International Master Instructor ,Tamalyn Dallal
and an Epilogue by Entreprenuer and Self Help Guru, Shelly Parris Williams.

"I've been doing a lot of soul-searching since reading this book and it
reminded me of why I dance. Thank you, Oriana!" - Zhor

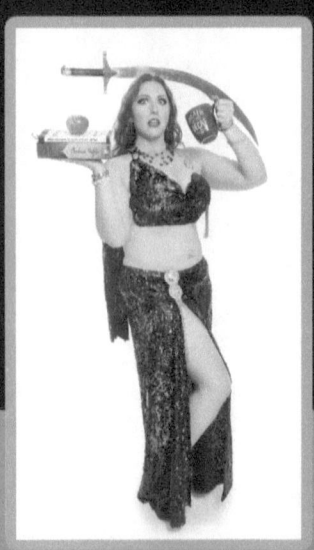

About the Author
Oriana is a professional Bellydancer, instructor, and Direc
of Midnight Lotus Dance Company; Tampa's only profess
Middle Eastern production company. She is a beloved
instructor and is regarded as an authority of Bellydance
in Tampa Bay. Oriana believes in diversity, education,
having a good laugh, and following your passion.

Photo by Carrie Meyer of The Dancer's Eye
Cover and Illustrations by Breanne Roberts

ISBN 978-0-359-90073-2

www.ingramcontent.com/pod-product-compliance
Lightning Source LLC
Chambersburg PA
CBHW030814180526
45163CB00003B/1285